RUTH

3,000 Years of Sleeping Prophecy
AWAKENED

by Diane A. McNeil

Plus Special Bonus Section
A Christian's Primer of Jewish Life and Customs

Copyright © 2005 by Diane A. McNeil

RUTH
3,000 Years of Sleeping Prophecy Awakened
by Diane A. McNeil

Printed in the United States of America

ISBN 1-59781-338-9

Unless otherwise indicated, Bible quotations are taken from the *King James Open Bible (Authorized King James Version)*, © 1985, by Thomas Nelson, Inc.

www.xulonpress.com

DEDICATION

I dedicate this labor of love to all the many Jewish friends and acquaintances God has privileged me to know and respect. You have taught me more than any book could ever contain. Without you there would be no story to tell. And, that is the story – the unique, God-ordained plan for *unity* between the Jewish people and true Christian believers. It is to you, the many beloved "Naomis" in my life, that I dedicate this book.

ACKNOWLEDGMENTS

This is extremely difficult, because when you've been writing something for ten years, you've shoved the manuscript in a many a face, anxious for some kind of feedback. So, to all of you, whether or not you wanted to read the manuscript, and whether or not your name appears here, I am forever indebted.

First, to my husband and family – I can only imagine how sick you must have gotten all those years hearing about Ruth – waiting until one more thing was done on Ruth – or, my promising to clean it when I figured out something else about Ruth – or, my wanting to have just one weekend to myself, and then Ruth would be finished. I have pronounced this book "finished" at least a dozen times. The truth is a book like this probably never gets finished. Thank you Ken, Chip, Scott, Adam, Candace, Rachel and Nathan for all the times you kept silent, and all the times you allowed Ruth to come before you.

To my parents: "Mother and Daddy, thank you for my upbringing. And, thank you for all the nights I went to bed hearing the two of you taking turns reading the Bible to each other. I love that Book, too."

A special thanks goes to my dear friend, Kathryn, for her love and encouragement, without whose contribution, this book would not be in print. May all your kindness come back to bless you.

To four very special editors, I give a loud round of applause: Jon, Mary Jane, Nancy and Tracy. If it weren't for you, the poor reader would be out there chasing a lot of rabbit trails. May you be exceedingly, abundantly blessed!

Also, I want to thank four gracious, Jewish ladies who read through the manuscript, critiquing the portions on Jewish tradition. I bless you Naomi, Anne, Shirley and Jami.

I offer special thanks to a strong team of prayer warriors who meet weekly to pray for Israel: Judy, Ann, Bubba and Jennifer. What is accomplished inside those four walls that one hour each week can only be measured in eternity. Thank you for the many prayers over this book.

To three dear pastor friends who never ceased to encourage and direct, I pray mighty blessings on you and your ministries: Bro. Boyd, Bro. Allen and Bro. Brown.

To an awesome map maker who has blessed my life and our little group here in Memphis (Christian Friends of Israel – Memphis) immeasurably. Thank you, Janie, for generously sharing your talent. May you be blessed beyond compare for your contribution.

To some special readers who were kind enough to be honest: Gordon, Pam, Wanda, Rachel, Roger, Ted, Sandy and Billie. I bless you and thank you.

Finally, I want to thank a dear, dear group who are not only my friends, but have been strong encouragers: Mary Jane, Nancy, Doyle, Miriam, Denise, Casey, Debra, Sharon, Susan and Ann.

May God give each of you a genuine reward for your invaluable contribution.

> In His service,
> Diane A. McNeil

TESTIMONIAL

April 10, 2005

Dear Diane:

I wanted to tell you what God has done in my life since the Eagles weekend getaway, hosted by our dear friend Debra.

On Sunday morning you shared with us from your study on the Book of Ruth. It was so powerful that it's changed my life. A love for Israel was birthed in my heart and in my spirit for God's Nation. The passion with which you shared about Israel has forever forged a passion in my own life for this great Nation. I knew when I left Reelfoot Lake, Tennessee, that I was changed. I came home and found myself being awakened in the night with a burden and a love for Israel that wasn't there until that weekend. I found myself weeping for this wonderful Nation. And, it didn't just happen one night, it was often. I told Debra, "Diane has *messed me up*. I find myself weeping for the Nation of Israel, and I find I have a love for her I didn't have before."

I could not understand what had happened to me until the weekend of April 9th, 2005. My brother, Efrain, decided to go to Lubbock, Texas, with his family to buy a shofar.* He is very gifted musically, and he just had to have one. They found a place called "King David's." He told me that when he entered the shop, he noticed the anointing of the Lord was very strong in that place. He said a lady approached him and asked if she could help him. My brother told her he was interested in buying a shofar. She had several, and he selected one, and told her he didn't know how to play it. As she started to show him, she stopped and said, "In the Name of Yeshua (Hebrew for Jesus), you will be playing the shofar in a week." Then, she told him, "Yahweh just said that He has directed your steps into this place." She asked my brother, "Do you know who you are?" He replied, "I think so." She asked his first name, and he said, "Efrain." Then, she asked his last name, and he said, "Rios." She took him to a computer, logged on to a website and said, "Read and learn who you are." Our last name is of direct Jewish descent. We are Sephardic Jews.**

My brother shared the above with me, and then I understood my love and the burden and passion for Israel. Because you see, Diane, it was several months before that that Yahweh directed your steps into my life, and I got *"messed up!"* I am indebted to you for all eternity. Thank you for sharing a part of you that has enriched my life.

In His service,
Dee Rios

*A ram's horn.
**A Jew of Spain and Portugal before the Inquisition.

TABLE OF CONTENTS

INTRODUCTION

It is with great fear and trembling that I share this material on the Book of Ruth. I know the seriousness of handling carefully the Word of God. James (3:1) warns that, because of his influence, a teacher will be judged more severely than others. In the New International Version, this verse says, "...*not many of you should presume to be teachers.*"

I never asked God for this assignment. I never desired to be a writer, and I certainly would never have chosen to write something for which I could potentially be "judged more severely." Also, this has not been an easy assignment. Over the past ten years of the writing of this book, I've begged God many times, often in tears, to stop me if this were not His work. And, when I'd come to one of those many roadblocks along the way, I'd dig my heels in and say, "God, if you don't help me with this one, then I can't go any further!" He always came to my rescue and gave the necessary understanding. He never stopped me; He never even allowed me to slow down. On the contrary, time and time again, He pressed me to keep going, not to let go and not to give up.

Satan told me many times, "You're stupid for doing this ... how dare you think you can write a Bible study!" And, you know, he was right ... but God! The giant, awesome, incomparable God who lives inside me can do amazing things with a simple "wife, grand-mother and homemaker." The more I pressed on, the more God continued to feed me through Scripture, Jewish friends, countless articles, commentaries and personal experiences.

This study is an allegorical approach to the Book of Ruth, meaning that each character in the story has a hidden or symbolic meaning. An allegory runs on two tracks simultaneously, with a description of one thing under the image of another. In the Book of Ruth, we have the story with which most of us are familiar, but we also see another story being played out ... one with a much broader, prophetic scope. There are many twists and turns along the way that at times may find you a bit stunned and shocked, or thrilled beyond words, or left, quite possibly, in tears.

No longer will this book be viewed as a simple, little love story with a predictable, "happily-ever-after" ending. Rather, it is a prophetic book of epic proportions. When opened fully, the Book of Ruth deals with one of today's most controversial issues: "Of what concern to me are Israel and the Jew?"

When confronted with the seriousness of the Book of Ruth, no longer will the *true* evangelical believer be able to side-step this "delicate subject." There can be no "straddling the fence." Just as this question is on the front burner of major world powers, even so, Israel and the Jew are on the forefront of God's agenda. On this all-important subject we will be held accountable, not only as a nation, but as the Church, and as individuals.

You now stand on the threshold of a journey that, hopefully, will leave you with a greater understanding and appreciation for the biblical design of Jewish/Gentile relations. In no other book of the Bible is this more clearly seen than in the Book of Ruth. And, at no other time in history has God allowed Ruth to be more transparent than in our day.

This work did not originate with me. The Source and Instigator of this book is God. It is literally material He taught me, line-by-line, and much of which I was required to experience first hand. I wrote it for one purpose only ... God called me to do it, and the only appropriate response was to obey.

A brief word about the layout and contents before getting started: There are twelve chapters that take you verse by verse through the Book of Ruth. Coinciding with the twelve chapters are twelve segments entitled, *"Did you Know?"* These deal with Jewish customs, traditions and feasts, and shed additional light on Ruth. They are interesting, informative and a valuable tool (not only for this study, but as a resource for those who work and interact with Jewish people). Rather than reading these segments as a unit, I urge you to read them in conjunction with the chapters. (For example, read segment one, "The Sabbath," at the end of Chapter One; segment two, "Kosher," at the end of Chapter Two, etc.) Also, there are numerous charts and a map at the end of the book (which are referenced in the text).

I pray God will open your mind's understanding as you study His precious Word through the Book of Ruth. May He richly bless you as you step back into history ... or quite possibly ***step forward into the future.***

Diane A. McNeil
dianemcneil@hotmail.com

ONE

"Bethlehem to Moab, Enemy Territory"
Ruth 1:1-2

This incredible journey began on Sunday morning, August 19, 1995. I was at home in bed with a severe case of tonsillitis. My husband, Ken, had gone to church. I had a fever, couldn't swallow, and was so miserable I honestly felt like dying. Suddenly, while lying there in my bed, I heard a voice deep in my spirit as clearly as any I'd ever heard audibly say, "Hi, my name is Ruth, and I'm meditative grocery stores." This was such a jolt. I completely lost all thoughts of my miserable sore throat. I jumped to my feet and went over to my desk and wrote down the perplexing words, then grabbed my Bible and crawled back in bed. I turned quickly with great anticipation to the Book of Ruth, firmly expecting to find something truly amazing – a treasure, a revelation from God!

I read through the entire book (just four chapters), and, to my disappointment, found nothing that I hadn't seen the other times I'd read it. But, I wasn't discouraged. I knew the Lord had spoken to me, and I told Him I wasn't giving up until I understood the meaning of that encounter.

Over the next few weeks and months, I read Ruth in every translation of the Bible I could get my hands on, and always with the same conclusion – nothing new. I combed studies, commentaries,

Bible dictionaries – still nothing. Undaunted, I decided to step back and take a different approach. I knew I was to be "meditating" on the Book of Ruth, but I had no idea what was meant by the "grocery stores" part. On a whim I picked up the phone and called my local grocery. I told the person at the other end that I was doing "a little study," and wanted to know how many different items they stocked on their shelves. To my astonishment, she told me, "30,000 normally and up to 50,000 for major holidays." That was shocking! I had no idea there were that many things in a grocery store! Immediately, I went to my own kitchen shelves to take inventory of my goods. I calculated, "If I have 500 items, then I have 1.67% of the 30,000 available. And, if I have 1,500 items (which sounded like a lot to me), then that's still only 5%." I thought, "Wow, percentage wise, I really don't have much at all *compared to what's available to me*!" Then, I realized what the Lord was trying to tell me. Just as I rarely venture beyond the norm of my daily shopping – same aisles, same items, same meals – the same is true for the Book of Ruth. He was telling me that I knew very little of the deep truths found in Ruth even though I had read it many, many times, because each time I read it with the same familiarity. Those treasures were available to me, but I would never find them unless I ventured beyond the norm, did some serious meditating in the Word, and viewed Ruth as a limitless supply of desirable (spiritual) goods readily available. I had to go to "unfamiliar shelves," select "items" totally foreign to me, bring them into my own life, and personally experience them.

I also came to understand that just as the items in my grocery store increased at major holidays (from 30,000 to 50,000), incredibly, when the Book of Ruth is studied in conjunction with the three major Jewish holidays, the information likewise multiplies.

How incredible of God to speak to me in such a unique, personal way – through a Gentile (Ruth), my own grocery store, and through meditating on the Word, which I love to do. That was how it all began, and though it's been a rather long journey, I wouldn't trade it for anything. I pray that many are called to take a new look at Ruth, to meditate on her timeless treasures, and dare to step outside their norm into the vast, waiting storehouse.

Verse 1. ***Now it came to pass in the days when the judges ruled, that there was a famine in the land. And a certain man of Bethlehem-judah went to sojourn in the country of Moab, he, and his wife, and his two sons.*** The times of the Judges were an embarrassing, black mark on Israel's history. As a matter of fact, our pastor recently preached through the Book of Judges, and when he got to the last three chapters he said, "Judges 19 thorough 21 are the sewer of the Scriptures; they are the dirtiest part of the Bible."[1] This is where our story begins.

There are several clues in this verse that point to the godlessness of that time. The first is the statement that "there was a famine in the land." There was never any reason for God's children to experience a famine. Listen to what God told the Israelites in Deuteronomy 11:13-17:

> *"And it shall come to pass, if ye shall hearken diligently unto my commandments which I command you this day, to love the Lord your God, and to serve him with all your heart and with all your soul, that I will give you the rain of your land in his due season, the first rain and the latter rain, that thou mayest gather in the corn, and thy wine, and thine oil. And I will send grass in thy fields for thy cattle, that thou mayest eat and be full. Take heed to yourselves, that your heart be not deceived, and ye turn aside, and serve other gods, and worship them; and then the Lord's wrath be kindled against you, and he shut up the heaven, that there be no rain, and that the land yield not her fruit; and lest ye perish quickly from off the good land which the Lord giveth you."*

In these verses God made it very clear that He would faithfully send the rain for their crops and cattle "if" they would love and serve Him with all their heart and soul. They failed over and over. God always honors His word. When they strayed from Him, He sent the promised famines. However, being a God of great compassion and tender mercy, when they repented and turned back, he faithfully delivered them from the famines and often sent abundant blessings.[2]

In order to reinforce this command, God told Moses to tell the Israelites to bind four specific Scriptures to their forehead and hand during their daily prayers[3] (an activity many Jewish males still perform today). One of those four Scriptures is the passage we quoted from Deuteronomy 11.[4] If they would just obey, there would never be a famine in the land.

Not only are we told in this first verse that there was a famine, but we also see this family leaving Bethlehem and going to the land of *Moab* – another red flag. Moab is enemy territory. It all began back in Genesis 12:1, when God told Abram to leave his father's house and go to a land He would show him. Abram obediently made the journey, accompanied by his nephew, Lot. In time, however, it seems hostility arose between the servants of Abram and Lot because of the needs of their large flocks. Abram told Lot they had to part ways and gave him first choice of the land. Lot chose the green fields near Sodom and Gomorrah, and Abram took what was left. You will recall that some time later, God pronounced judgment on the cities of Sodom and Gomorrah, and sent word to Lot and his family to flee, commanding them not to look back. Lot's wife couldn't resist the temptation, and when she disobeyed, God turned her into a pillar of salt. Lot and his two daughters continued on and settled in caves nearby. After some time, the two daughters decided they would never be allowed to leave that place, marry or have children, so they took matters into their own hands. They schemed to get their father drunk, have sexual relations with him and start their own families. Their plan worked and both got pregnant. The oldest named her son Moab (father of the Moabites), meaning "from the mother's father" (see Chart #1), and the youngest named her son Ben-Ammi (father of the Ammonites), meaning "son of my people" (Genesis 19:30-38).

It is to this land of Moab (the land of the descendants of Lot, the bitter enemies of the descendants of Abraham) that this family flees because of the famine. Moab, what a bizarre place of refuge for a Jewish family!

Verse 2. *And the name of the man was Elimelech, and the name of his wife Naomi, and the name of his two sons Mahlon and Chilion, Ephrathites of Bethlehem-judah. And they came into the country of Moab and continued there.* Early in my study, the recurring thought playing over and over in my head was that every time I'd heard this book preached or taught, it was always said that Naomi was a picture of Israel, Ruth a picture of the Church and Boaz Jesus. "That being so," I thought, "why couldn't God do it with *every* character in this book? Why would He single out just a few?" I felt I was limiting God to think He could give dual roles to only a few, and not to all. I then began looking for the parallel role of each character. (Remember, an allegory is a story in which people, things and happenings have a hidden, or symbolic, meaning. Allegories are used for teaching.)

In this verse we meet the first four players: Elimelech, Naomi, Mahlon and Chilion. If Naomi is, indeed, a picture of Israel, then who are the husband and two sons, allegorically? The first thing I felt I had to do to unravel this mystery was to find out the Hebrew meaning of their names.

Elimelech in Hebrew means "to me shall kingship come," or "out of me a king shall come." I knew if Naomi was portrayed as Israel, then Elimelech, her husband, could only be God because Isaiah 54:5 says:

> *"For thy Maker is thine <u>husband</u>; the Lord of hosts is his name; and thy Redeemer the Holy One of Israel; The God of the whole earth shall he be called."*

Interestingly, several of the Jewish commentaries I read were very critical of Elimelech and his harsh treatment of Naomi, Mahlon and Chilion, suggesting he was the one responsible for their leaving Bethlehem. The Midrash (Jewish commentary) says Elimelech's name signified his arrogant attitude. "He would boast: 'to me shall kingship come. . .' "Elimelech considered himself to be a prominent individual, always boasting 'to me shall kingship come.' Therefore, he should have considered the consequences of his desertion of the land – and so, he deserved to be punished."[5] I thought, "If Elimelech, is a picture of God, then these are some very serious charges."

The wife's name was Naomi, meaning "my pleasantness." The two sons were Mahlon, whose name means "weakling," and Chilion, meaning "sickly."

Allegorically, who were these two sons? They were very intriguing and not as easy to identify as Elimelech and Naomi, but once God revealed them to me, it was incredibly exciting, and I knew this journey was well on its way. These two weakling/sickly sons represent two equally weakling/sickly periods in Israel's history – the times of the Judges and the Kings. When I discovered who they were, I immediately went to Scripture to see if there was any correlation between the deaths of the two sons and the "demise" of the Judges and Kings. What I discovered was astounding.

Samson was considered the last major Judge in Israel. You know the story of Samson's life, but do you know the story of how the times of the Judges came to an end with him? In Judges 16:21 we read,

> *"But the Philistines took him, and put out his eyes, and brought him down to Gaza, and bound him with fetters of brass; and he did grind in the prison house."*

(The blind eyes, fetters of brass and being taken into captivity are major clues.)

Let's now go forward to the same time period for the Kings. Zedekiah was the last King to reign before the fall of Jerusalem. Note how he was removed from Israel. In II Kings 25:5-7 we are told:

> *"And the army of the Chaldees pursued after the king, and overtook him in the plains of Jericho: and all his army were scattered from him. So they took the king, and brought him up to the king of Babylon to Riblah; and they gave judgment upon him. And they slew the sons of Zedekiah before his eyes, and put out the eyes of Zedekiah, and bound him with*

fetters of brass, and carried him to Babylon."

The irony of all of this is that they had been forewarned of God's requirements and the resulting consequences. Joshua 23:12-13, says:

> *Else if ye do in any wise go back, and cleave unto the remnant of these nations, even these that remain among you, and shall make marriages with them, and go in unto them, and they to you: Know for a certainty that the Lord your God will no more drive out any of these nations from before you; but they shall be snares and traps unto you, and scourges in your sides, and thorns in your eyes, until ye perish from off this good land which the Lord your God hath given you.*

The "Judges" and the "Kings" died in enemy territory, blind and in bondage. Both failed the one dependent upon them – Israel. Both left her totally exposed, vulnerable and defenseless.

TWO

"Ten Years in Moab and Death"
Ruth 1:3-7

Elimelech_____ † Naomi _____ †Mahlon _____ †

Chilion _____ †

In Chapter One we said that approaching the Book of Ruth allegorically meant each character has a hidden or parallel role. At the beginning of each chapter the players will be listed in the order of their appearance in the story. You may want to pencil in the corresponding role in the space provided to keep these parallels in focus. (Elimelech is allegorically God; Naomi, Israel; Mahlon, the Judges; and Chilion, the Kings.)

In the previous chapter, we also discussed how the two periods of the Judges and the Kings ended. Judge Samson and King Zedekiah both had their eyes put out, were bound in bronze shackles and taken to foreign countries as captives. There were a combined total of 40 Judges and Kings, with the periods lasting approximately 400 years each. Could these numbers, 40 and 400, have significance?

In the Appendix at the back of the book under "Hebrew

Numerology," you will find a list of many of the major numbers and their meanings, according to Jewish scholars. We are told that the number 40 (400 will be the same) means a time of "probation and divine testing." How did these "40" Judges and Kings, ruling "400" years measure up during their probation and testing period? Unfortunately, they failed their test miserably, leaving Israel defenseless. Could it be that what was said of the Judges and Kings will also be said of the two weakling/sickly sons, Mahlon and Chilion? Will they, too, prove to be to Naomi what the Judges and Kings were to Israel? Will the sons die in enemy territory leaving Naomi defenseless?

There is another interesting element concerning the Book of Ruth, and that is its unique placement in our Bible. We have the Book of Judges, followed by Ruth, then I and II Samuel and I and II Kings. Originally, both Samuel and Kings were one book. (I and II Samuel tell of the rise and reign of King David, and I and II Kings give the details of the other Kings.) Thus, we have the little Book of Ruth, the book of love, hope, selflessness, faith and belief wedged between two godless, self-centered, legalistic periods in Israel's history: the Judges and the Kings.

Verse 3. *And Elimelech Naomi's husband died; and she was left, and her two sons.* When I came to this verse, I thought, "Lord, I know you're leading me to do this parallel study, so how in the world can it ever be said that Elimelech dies when he represents you, the God of all creation? That just can't be!" And, I knew if God didn't make this perfectly clear to me *from Scripture* that I could never go any further.

I called a dear Jewish friend who was born and raised in Israel, and whose primary language is Hebrew, and asked her to please go to her Tenach (TAH NAHK – the Hebrew word for the Jewish Scripture – the Old Testament), look up this verse in Ruth and tell me what "died" meant. She looked it up and said, "Died means died." I said, "No, it can't," and she said, "Well, it does." But, I knew there had to be an answer, and I had to find it. I poured over commentaries and word studies, and couldn't find what I knew was there. One day I went to a Christian book store determined to look at everything on their shelves, and as I was standing in a corner holding Strong's Concordance (which I had at home and had looked at numerous times), there it was – the missing puzzle piece. It had been there all the time, but I just hadn't seen it. The Hebrew word "mooth," translated "died," means "to kill or be dead," true … but what I had overlooked was this word could be used *literally* or *figuratively*.[6] Literally, in our story Elimelech died, but, the allegorical Elimelech (God) *died figuratively* to Israel.

Let's look at that time in Israel's history when this "death" occurred. God was to be the only "Ruler" over Israel. A Covenant to this effect was made between God and Israel during her desert wanderings. In Exodus 19:3-6, God told Moses to speak to the children of Israel and tell them:

> *Ye have seen what I did unto the Egyptians, and how I bare you on eagles' wings, and brought you unto myself. Now therefore, if ye will obey my voice indeed, and keep my covenant, then ye shall be a peculiar treasure unto me above all people: for all the earth is mine: And ye shall be unto me a <u>kingdom</u> of priests, and an holy nation. These are the words which thou shalt speak unto the children of Israel."*

Moses took these words back to the people (Exodus 19:8), and they all responded in unison: *"All that the Lord hath spoken we will do."* With these words they entered into a binding covenant with God, and they became His *Kingdom*. (Remember that Elimelech's name means, "to me shall kingship come.") God didn't want lands or provinces or countries to rule; those already belonged to Him. He wanted a willing people who would be a peculiar treasure unto him above all people. Sadly, time passed and the Israelites began to stray from their commitment to God.

After the deaths of Moses and Joshua, God raised up Judges to be "deliverers" during particular crises. These Judges were never meant to be "rulers;" that was God's place. However, listen to what the Israelites told Judge Gideon in Judges 8:22-23:

Rule thou over us, both thou, and thy son, and thy son's son also: for thou hast delivered us from the hand of Midian. And Gideon said unto them, I will not rule over you, neither shall my son rule over you: the Lord shall rule over you.

Gideon reprimanded the people for their sinful request and reminded them that the Lord only was to rule over them. They were in a binding covenant with God, and nothing had changed that covenant.

Unfortunately, they continued this rebelliousness. In I Samuel 8:4-7, the elders of Israel went to the Prophet Samuel and told him he was old, they didn't like his sons, and they wanted him to appoint a king to rule over them like they saw in all the surrounding nations. Samuel was very upset with the people and went to God with their demand. God told him (verse 7):

Hearken unto the voice of the people in all that they say unto thee: for they have not rejected thee, but they have rejected me, that I should not reign over them.

God told Samuel to give them what they wanted. God gives man free will; we are free to make our own choices – even if those choices don't include Him. They rejected God as their supreme Ruler.

Thinking allegorically, Scripture tells of a time when Israel is *widowed.* You can't be a widow unless a death occurs. Isaiah tells of Messiah's promise to restore the "widowed" Israel. Listen to verse four of Isaiah 54:

Fear not; for thou shalt not be ashamed: neither be thou confounded; for thou shalt not be put to shame: for thou shalt forget the shame of thy youth, and shalt not remember the reproach of thy widowhood any more.

This verse says Israel's widowed condition will not last forever.

Something phenomenal is going to happen, and she will never again remember the shame of that time in her life.

In our story we are only told that Elimelech died. We don't know any of the circumstances. However, we do know the circumstances for the *figurative* "death" of God to Israel. Ezekiel tells us this heart-wrenching story. In Ezekiel 9, 10 and 11, we are told how God took the prophet in a vision from the land of his captivity to Jerusalem to witness this "death." From Ezekiel's vantage point overlooking the Temple Mount, he saw the Glory of the Lord rise from above the cherubim inside the Holy of Holies (9:3). He then watched as the Glory moved eastward to the threshold of the Temple and paused (10:3). Next, he saw the Glory move further East and stop at the entrance to the East Gate (10:19), and finally, he watched as it stopped at the Mount of Olives (11:23). Ezekiel was then whisked back to Babylon. How he must have grieved as he witnessed the Glory of God – the incomparable God of all creation, the Husband of Israel (Isaiah 54:5) – rise from the midst of His chosen people and move slowly out of sight. The Eternal King, "figuratively" died to Israel that day by popular demand. He stepped aside so earthly kings could take their reign over His peculiar treasure.

Verse 4a: *And they* (the two sons) *took them wives of the women of Moab; the name of the one was Orpah, and the name of the other Ruth.* With Elimelech out of the picture, the two sons marry women from the pagan country of Moab. What did it take to make a marriage in that culture? The usual procedure was for the groom's father to go to the prospective bride's father and make the arrangements. Both the bride and her father received wedding gifts. Women were considered liabilities to the parents because they raised the girls and then gave them away, getting nothing in return for their years of investment. So, tradition was that the father of the groom would give the father of the bride gifts to "reimburse him." In addition, the groom's father would often give gifts to the bride, as would the groom. Elimelech, however, is no longer present to make these arrangements, so we have to assume that Naomi handled the details.

We have in Scripture the arrangements for a similar marriage that took place at approximately the same time period. Let's look there to better understand this custom. In Judges 14:1-3, we read of Samson's marriage proposal to a non-Jew.

> *And Samson went down to Timnath, and saw a woman in Timnath of the daughters of the Philistines. And he came up, and told his father and his mother, and said, I have seen a woman in Timnath of the daughters of the Philistines: now therefore get her for me to wife. Then his father and his mother said unto him, Is there never a woman among the daughters of thy brethren, or among all my people, that thou goest to take a wife of the uncircumcised Philistines? And Samson said unto his father, Get her for me; for she pleaseth me well.*

Who could refuse Samson? Apparently, not even his father or his mother.

We cannot imagine the agony of this family to have their son *demand* a wife from an enemy, pagan nation. It wasn't a small matter then, and it's not a small matter now, thousands of years later. Even in today's society, there are often serious consequences when a Jew and a non-Jew marry. Let me tell you of the marriage of two personal friends. They met at work and fell in love. She was from an observant Jewish family and he was from a Christian family. Her parents forbade her to marry him, but she disobeyed. After the marriage her family held a funeral service for her. She was "figuratively" dead to them. She told me that her family took down all her pictures, and put her as far away from them, mentally and physically, as they could. In a traditional Jewish home, when there is a literal death, the family will sit "sheva" for seven days ("sheva" means seven in Hebrew), receiving family and friends who wish to pay their respects. I do not know if my friend's family actually sat *sheva* for her, but some Jewish families even go to this extreme when there is intermarriage. Just as my friends' marriage was not acceptable in today's culture, and Samson's not acceptable in his, so the marriages of Elimelech's sons could not have been a desirable thing for that family.

Verses 4b and 5. *And they dwelled there about ten years. And Mahlon and Chilion died also both of them; and the woman was left of her two sons and her husband.* After I read through Ruth many times, I became keenly aware that the number ten kept surfacing all throughout the story. This verse reveals the first ten. I found it interesting that the number ten, according to the Hebrew scholars, meant the "measure of *human responsibility*."[7] It is also a time of *special testing*. In addition, "ten people constitute a congregation in the synagogue and must be present at a nuptial blessing."[8] Ten represents a *quorum* – all that's required. After a young boy's bar mitzvah, he is eligible to be counted in the quorum. (See the number ten in Hebrew Numerology in the Appendix.)

Our story tells us that this Jewish family dwelt in Moab about "ten" years. During that time all three men died. If this ten signifies human responsibility and special testing, then there can be no doubt someone failed the test miserably.

These ten years brought great changes for Naomi. She is now a widow with no male covering (no authority figure over her). This was an extremely humiliating position. In that society she was now considered a liability, a charity case. She was dependent on others for her livelihood. She couldn't even claim Elimelech's estate, but had to hold it in trust for a male heir, an option seemingly no longer available to her.

Verse 6. *Then she* (Naomi) *arose with her daughters in law, that she might return from the country of Moab: for she had heard in the country of Moab how that the Lord had visited his people in giving them bread.* Naomi, living in the pagan, enemy country of Moab, hears of the Lord's faithfulness to His people back in Israel. The famine was over, and the land was once again producing food. How did she get the news? Did a "Moabite" have to tell her what was going on in *her* own homeland? Did she hear it from a distant traveler? How sad that she had to receive the news second hand. "Naomi, how did you get so far from home, and what price did you have to pay?"

Verse 7. *Wherefore she went forth out of the place where she was, and her two daughters in law with her; and they went on the way to return unto the land of Judah.* She knew this day would come, but did she ever dream that it would be ten years in coming? And, could she have ever imagined that it would be like this? When their little family left Bethlehem so long ago, was her head filled with thoughts of returning soon, their sons marrying good Jewish girls, and Elimelech and her settling down into their happy roles as grandparents? "It just wasn't supposed to turn out like this."

Naomi, Orpah and Ruth pack their belongings and set out on the road that leads to Bethlehem, Judah. What should have been an exciting, happy day for Naomi – returning home – was probably more like a funeral dirge with the elder widow flanked by two much younger widows.

As embarrassing and humiliating as this trip would be for Naomi (returning with Moabite "daughters" rather than Israeli sons), there had to have been a sigh of relief that the time had finally come. At last she could return to her God, her people, her family, her home, her customs and her traditions. But, have we ever stopped to consider what this trip would mean for Orpah and Ruth? The things Naomi longed to regain were the very things Orpah and Ruth would relinquish. With every step they took, Orpah and Ruth left further behind their gods, their people, their family, their home, their customs and their traditions. Who can understand the pain and agony of such a journey?

THREE

"Orpah Leaves, Ruth Cleaves"
Ruth 1:8-17

Elimelech_____ ✝Naomi _____ ✝Mahlon _____ ✝

Chilion _____ ✝

Verse 8. *And Naomi said unto her two daughters in law, Go, return each to her mother's house: the Lord deal kindly with you, as ye have dealt with the dead, and with me.* Back in verse six, Naomi, Orpah and Ruth made preparations to leave Moab. In verse seven they started on their journey, but here in verse eight, it seems Naomi has a change of heart. In leaving the land of Moab, does she become concerned with the stark cultural differences facing her daughters-in-law? Or, is she contemplating the difficulty in returning a widow, compounded with two widows along side of her? Maybe she's dreading the embarrassment of everyone seeing two Moabite "daughters" in place of her two Jewish sons. Or, perhaps the three of them have stopped to say their good-byes to the families of Orpah and Ruth, and she can't bear watching the pain of separation, a pain she knows all too well. These girls will likely never see their families again. Whatever the reasons, Naomi changes her mind and tells the girls to go back to their homes.

These girls have obviously been wonderful wives and daughters-in-law. Naomi, in telling them to go back to their homes, speaks a blessing over both of her "daughters." She asks the Lord, her Lord – the God of Israel – to be as kind in His dealings with them as they have been with her and her sons.

Verse 9. *The Lord grant you that ye may find rest, each of you in the house of her husband. Then she kissed them; and they lifted up their voice, and wept.* In addition to Naomi's prayer for kindness, she also asks the Lord of Israel to give them other husbands and homes. Loud weeping follows. Is it possible for a Moabite woman who has been married and intimate with an *Israeli* – that enemy nation – to nonchalantly blend back into her own people and society with no repercussions? Such intermarriages would certainly have caused societal prejudice against a Moabite girl. Naomi compassionately asks her merciful God to give them rest in the home of another husband. She asks that they be given a second chance. The Hebrew word for "rest" in this verse means peace and consolation. She entreats God by His mercy to give them peace and consolation with another husband and another home.

Are the two blessings Naomi speaks over Orpah and Ruth in verses 8 and 9 ever realized? We know what happens to Ruth, but what about Orpah? Do we have any clues?

It's been amazing to watch all the things God has put in my path concerning Ruth during these ten years of study. He knew I needed a lot of help and much reassurance along the way. One such affirmation came by way of a Jewish friend who brought me a copy of one of the leading newspapers in Israel, *The Jerusalem Post*, which ran an article on June 7, 1997, featuring Ruth. My friend thought I would enjoy seeing it. Note this one sentence from that article: "There is Ruth and there is Orpah, who both have amazing strengths . . . Orpah, who turned her back on Naomi, was the great-grandmother of Goliath, and Ruth, the great-grandmother of David."[9] Amazing! David and Goliath – who would ever have imagined?

This was also cited in an article appearing in *Israel My Glory* magazine. "According to both the *Encyclopedia Judaica* and the *Jewish Encyclopedia*, Ruth, as recorded in the biblical account, went on to become the great-grandmother of King David (4:13-17). ...Orpah, on the other hand, returned to Moab, forsook the God of Israel, and worshipped the gods of the Moabites. She is identified with Harafu, the mother of four Philistine giants, one of whom was Goliath."[10]

Jewish historians teach that indeed both Orpah and Ruth had other husbands and homes. But, oh, the consequences of the choice they made!

Orpah's name means "the nape of the neck," because Jewish scholars say she turned her back on Naomi. Ruth's name means "friend" or "female companion," because of her love and commitment to Naomi.

Verse 10. *And they* (the girls) *said unto her* (Naomi)*, Surely we will return with thee unto thy people.* These three have no doubt cried many tears together in the past few years. Tears are no stranger to any of them. Once again weeping overtakes the three (verse 9). Orpah and Ruth by this time are probably more like sisters, rather than sisters-in-law, because of the similar, tragic events affecting both of them. Naomi, also, must certainly be dearer than most mothers-in-law because she, too, is a member of this "painful society of widowhood."

The tears flow. Naomi, Orpah and Ruth are at a critical juncture in their lives, one in which each must make a "life-changing" decision. Naomi is firm in her resolve to go back to Bethlehem, and Orpah and Ruth must now choose whether or not they will go with her or remain in the land of Moab. Naomi says to them, "Stay," to which they respond, "Surely, we will return with thee unto thy people."

Verse 11 – 13. *And Naomi said, Turn again, my daughters: why will ye go with me? Are there yet any more sons in my womb, that they may be your husbands?* (v. 12) *Turn again, my daughters, go your way; for I am too old to have an husband. If I should say, I have hope, if I should have an husband also to night, and should also bear sons;* (v. 13) *Would ye tarry for them till they were grown? Would ye stay for them from having husbands? Nay,*

35

my daughters; for it grieveth me much for your sakes that the hand of the Lord is gone out against me. What does this bizarre line of questioning mean? Why at this late stage in the game would Naomi mention having another husband, giving birth to more sons and them growing up and marrying Orpah and Ruth? What a seemingly ridiculous and inconceivable proposal she's making. Let's be realistic here. Let's put everything into perspective by doing a little math. Say that Naomi married around 18 and had her two sons a few years later. If Mahlon and Chilion were in their early to mid-twenties when they died, that would make Naomi about forty-five to fifty – not exactly prime time for starting a new family. Not only that, but she has to get the husband first. And, what about Orpah and Ruth? They are possibly in their late teens or early twenties. What enticement is there for these young women to wait until they are 40, or so, to get another husband and start their family? (And, wouldn't these new "husbands" be more like kid brothers rather than marriage partners?) All of this seems preposterous, doesn't it? But, not only is it not preposterous, this scenario is God's design.

Verses 11-13 give us our first glimpse of a law known as "levirate law." Levir in Latin means "brother-in-law." God instituted levirate law in Deuteronomy 25:5-10. Verses 5 and 6 tell us:

> *"If brethren dwell together, and one of them die, and have no child, the wife of the dead shall not marry without unto a stranger: her husband's brother shall go in unto her, and take her to him to wife, and perform the duty of an husband's brother unto her. And it shall be, that the firstborn which she beareth shall succeed in the name of his brother which is dead, that his name be not put out of Israel.*

What we see in levirate law is God's plan: (1) to insure that the land of Israel continues within the family to which it was given, and (2) to provide the necessary male covering to the one society would otherwise expel. A widow with no male covering (no authority figure over her), was reduced to charity.

Naomi knows this law. Apparently, she's convicted about it

because of what she says, but she's not convicted enough to play by the "rules." She has given up all hope. In these three verses (11, 12 and 13), she speaks much about *her* impossibility to "provide" for Orpah and Ruth, but never once does she leave room for God's ability. Levirate law says the widow is to marry one of her husband's brothers, bear children, and thus maintain an unbroken line for the deceased. Does Naomi really think that her situation is too great an obstacle for God? What about Abraham and Sarah? Sarah was 90 when she conceived. And, according to God's timeline, she was right in the middle of her prime – right where she needed to be to show forth His power and His majesty. If Naomi were willing and would yield herself to Him, she, too, could be used to show forth His might and miracles. Sadly, though, Naomi is not willing. Her personal *famine* still rages unabated.

For the first time Naomi hints where the real problem lies. After this self-centered, pitiful performance about her helplessness in finding a husband and having sons for her "daughters" to marry, she says, "It is more bitter for me than for you, because the Lord's hand has gone out against *me!*" Do you remember our discussion back in verse three where the Jewish scholars blamed Elimelech for taking Naomi off to Moab? Does Naomi seem like the type person who would take the blame for something she *didn't* do? Never once does she bring a charge against Elimelech. Not one time does she blame him, and she could so easily do it because he's not there to defend himself. She makes it quite clear that the problem lies between her and God, and this problem has now spilled over into the lives of these two young women. We are mindless to ever think that we alone bear the consequences of our sins. The sinner most certainly pays the price, but all too often there are innocent bystanders who are drawn into the wake of the sinner's offense.

Verse 14. *And they lifted up their voice, and wept again: and Orpah kissed her mother in law; but Ruth clave unto her.* In the midst of their weeping, Orpah kisses Naomi, and then turns her back. Most of us think that this was the logical, most practical thing to do. Why shouldn't she? Her husband is dead; she's free. However, there is a major problem with Orpah's decision to leave

Naomi. She's going back on a commitment she made in verse 10 where both she and Ruth vowed together, *"Surely we will return with thee unto thy people."* Listen to what Jesus said about such people in Luke 9:62:

> *And Jesus said unto him, No man, having put his hand to the plough, and looking back, is fit for the kingdom of God.*

Lot's wife "put her hand to the plow" when she left Sodom and Gomorrah. She, like Orpah, was out on the road headed in the right direction; then she looked back. And, consider the effect this had on her two daughters. Those daughters would never have gotten their father drunk and slept with him if their mother had been around. They were pulled into the wake of their mother's sin. Consider Judas Iscariot. He also "put his hand to the plow" when Jesus called him to be a disciple, but in the end he kissed Jesus and turned his back. Orpah, in verse 10, set her hand to the plow. She said "Surely (of a certainty) I will..." Now, according to the words of Jesus, she is not fit for the kingdom of God because she turns back.

Who does Orpah portray in our allegorical approach to the Book of Ruth? We said in the beginning that Ruth is spoken of as a picture of true believers, the Church. But, if Ruth represents the Church, then who does Orpah represent? Naomi said both were kind to their husbands and to her. Orpah must have been a "good" person, but who is she in her counter role? She's "The World." Matthew 13 perfectly describes her in the parable of the seed. Jesus taught in this parable the reasons why some seeds don't "take hold" (verses 18-22). He says it is for lack of spiritual discernment; being overcome by trouble and persecution; or deluded by worries and wealth. Orpah had every opportunity as did Ruth. The great divide came when Orpah succumbed to the cares of the world. She could not let go of Moab. She walked by sight and Ruth by faith.

Verse 15. *And she* (Naomi) *said, Behold, thy sister in law is gone back unto her people, and unto her gods: return thou after thy sister in law.* This verse is one of the most condemning for

Naomi in all the Book of Ruth. Orpah has gone, but to Ruth Naomi says, "Your sister-in-law has gone back to her home and *her gods*, go back with her." How could Naomi, whose God is the one and only true God, ever say, "Go back to *your gods?*" Who are the gods of Moab? II Kings 3:26-27 gives us an alarming look at these gods.

> *And when the king of Moab saw that the battle was too sore for him, he took with him seven hundred men that drew swords, to break through even unto the king of Edom: but they could not. Then he took his eldest son that should have reigned in his stead, and offered him for a burnt offering upon the wall. And there was great indignation against Israel: and they departed from him, and returned to their own land.*

This is to whom Naomi tells Ruth to return – a god who requires child sacrifices. After ten years in this godless country and three horrendous deaths, Naomi's spiritual famine continues unabated.

Verse 16. *And Ruth said, Entreat me not to leave thee, or to return from following after thee: for whither thou goest, I will go; and where thou lodgest, I will lodge: thy people shall be my people, and thy God my God:* Ruth set her hand to the plow, her face toward Bethlehem and no amount of coaxing by Naomi is going to dislodge her from her resolve. In this verse she turns her back permanently on her Moabite birth place, her people and her gods.

This verse and the one following are completely out of character with Ruth's response to Naomi on every other occasion. Here, we sense almost a tone of rebuke from the younger to the elder. She details the vow to which she is making. She says, "If you are on the move, so am I; if you're stationary, I am too; your people of Israel are now my people, and Jehovah God is now my God."

Ruth continues in verse 17. *Where thou diest, will I die, and there will I be buried: the Lord do so to me, and more also, if aught but death part thee and me.* This vow (verses 16 and 17) covers every avenue of life from this time forward until both she and Naomi are laid to rest. And, make no mistake; this is a vow! She says, in essence, "From this moment forward, I will be your ever-constant companion; nothing will separate us. Even in death you will not be rid of me, because your final resting place will also be my final resting place."

There's an interesting side note pertaining to burials in Israel. When Ken and I were there in 1996, we were shown a shallow, open cave which was a small burial plot. The height of the opening looked to be only about 3 or 4 feet and maybe about 6 feet in depth. Inside were many small boxes, some even stacked on top of each other. We were told that after a year, the families would return to the burial site, take the bones from the completely decomposed body, and then place all the bones neatly into one of these small boxes. In that way entire families could be buried together in a relatively small, confined area. Possibly in this verse Ruth is saying that her final destination will be in the box right beside her beloved mother-in-law.

Ruth, a young woman, just committed herself for the rest of her life – her entire lifetime – to a rather bitter, aging woman who proclaimed that she has nothing more to offer in life. This vow Ruth makes is all-inclusive, the implications of which most of us fail to fully comprehend. Many of us can quote Ruth 1:16, but rarely do we ever finish the rest of the vow in verse 17.

> (v. 16) *And Ruth said, Entreat me not to leave thee, or to return from following after thee: for whither thou goest, I will go; and where thou lodgest, I will lodge: thy people shall be my people, and they God my God:* (v. 17) *Where thou diest, will I die, and there will I be buried: the Lord do so to me, and more also, if aught but death part thee and me.*

There are actually two vows in these verses, one from Ruth to Naomi and one from Ruth to the God of Israel – not a small matter. Her vow to Naomi stated that nothing – no matter the circumstance – would ever separate her deliberate attachment to Naomi. Her vow to God was that if at any time she failed to keep the vow to Naomi, then God was to step in and "do so to her, and more also." The

Hebrew translation for this phrase is, "May Jehovah deal with me and so may he be severe..."[11] In other words, she would be Naomi's constant companion, and if for some reason she went back on her word, then God was to deal severely with her. What a powerful, frightening (no gray areas) vow she makes! Under this vow *Naomi has no obligations.* It is a one-sided vow. All responsibilities lie with Ruth. What made Ruth speak such extreme words? Why did she feel the necessity to close herself in like this? She left herself no options – no way out. She has fully surrendered her life to Naomi, and the Overseer of this unconditional surrender is none other than the God of Abraham, Isaac and Jacob.

If, indeed, in the Book of Ruth Naomi is a picture of Israel and Ruth the Church, the true believers, then what are we to make of this vow?

When I was working on this portion of the manuscript, some Jewish friends from B'rit Hadasha Synagogue (a Messianic Jewish Synagogue) called Ken and me and asked us to come hear a guest speaker they were having from Israel. The man's name was Dan Juster. Dr. Juster is a believing Jew with Tikkun Ministries out of Gaithersburg, Maryland. We went that evening, and I was very intrigued with his message, so I bought one of his books. The book is entitled Israel, the Church and the Last Days (which Dr. Juster co-authored with Keith Intrater). I want to quote just a few excerpts from the book that I believe are pertinent to this passage in Ruth.

> "God is restoring and bringing into position both the Church and Israel. They are supposed to work together as a team. How God longs for these two to cooperate and come together. Israel needs the protection of intercessory prayer from the believers. In fact, it is the good things going on among Gentile Christians that attracts the Jew to salvation. As the Gentile Christians humble themselves, the blindness on the Jews, keeping them from receiving Yeshua (the Hebrew name of Jesus) will be removed, and the Jews will be saved."[12]

What Dr. Juster was saying was exactly what I was beginning to see unfold in the Book of Ruth. He said Israel *needed* the Church because the Church would play a key role in Israel's coming to faith in Messiah. If, in the Book of Ruth, allegorically, Naomi is a picture of Israel, and Ruth the Church, then what are we to make of such a vow? God knew it was absolutely essential for this relationship to stay intact, both literally in our story and allegorically in the parallel realm. The Book of Ruth reveals how God will use both Naomi (Israel) and Ruth (the Church) – two impoverished widows in need of a redeemer – to bring the true Redeemer to each other. This wasn't a hasty, youthful vow Ruth made without weighing the consequences. It was the heart and design of God Almighty from the foundation of the world to meld these two "lives" together in order that each might find the life-giving salvation.

Immediately after this revelation about unity between Israel and the Church, another Jewish friend loaned me a book by a gentile Christian, entitled Our Father Abraham. Consider what the author, Dr. Marvin Wilson, says on this same subject.

> "In Romans 11, Paul warns those who have come to faith out of gentile backgrounds not to 'boast' (v. 18) or become 'arrogant' (v. 20). They (the Gentiles) are but wild olive branches grafted into the olive tree (Israel, v. 24), allowed by God's goodness to 'share in the nourishing sap from the olive root' (v. 17). ... Paul uses this symbol of the living and growing olive tree to show that the destinies of faithful Jews and Gentiles are inextricably bound together. ... While ... Romans 11 depicts the unity of two peoples, Jews and Gentiles, their relationship has proved historically to be the opposite. The Church never seriously heeded Paul's warning to stand in awe, to 'be afraid' (Romans 11:20). Little did Paul realize, however, that his words of warning to the non-Jewish world about boastfulness and superiority would go largely unheeded. ... after Paul's time, the church would be virtually severed from its Jewish roots."[13]

What Paul says in these verses from Romans 11 is that we Gentiles (the wild olive branches) are *privileged* to be grafted into the olive tree. Paul says that in God's goodness to us, He grafted us in, and we now have Jewish roots. Never before did I think of myself as having such a personal, Jewish connection.

God wants us to understand this marvelous *mystery*, and I believe He wants us to understand it individually as well as corporately (the Church). Allow me to share my own personal testimony. One day I was in the car running errands and listening to WCRV Christian radio. An announcement came on saying B'rit Hadasha Messianic Jewish Congregation (about whom I knew nothing at the time) was having a Passover Seder, and the public was invited. The word "Passover" I understood, but didn't have a clue what a "Seder" was. However, the whole thing sounded very fascinating. Then, the part that cinched it for me was that it was going to be held on April 10th! That just happens to be my birthday. A few days later Ken said to me, "Honey, your birthday's coming up, what do you want to do?" He was shocked when I said I wanted to go to a Passover Seder. My husband is wonderful and a little indulging, so he "reluctantly" agreed to go. We went, and it was marvelous. That was one of those spiritual markers in my life never to be forgotten, and though time has passed, the warmth of that evening will never be lost.

A couple of years later, I was praying late one night, and was shocked when I distinctly heard the Lord say in my spirit, "B'rit Hadasha." I thought, "Wow, that's strange," but just figured God wanted me to pray for them, and I did and forgot all about it. The next day Ken called to ask me to meet him for lunch to sign some papers. When we walked into the restaurant, my eyes immediately were drawn to the corner of the room where the Rabbi from B'rit Hadasha who had hosted the Passover Seder sat. I told Ken what had happened the night before during my prayer time. He just shrugged it off, but I knew something God-sized was about to take place.

The restaurant had one of those long salad bars, and after giving the waitress our drink orders, we went over to make our salads. Ken (my Southern gentleman) was first in line, I was next, and then the Rabbi "just happened" to come up and stand in line behind me. I knew God had orchestrated the whole affair, and as uptight as I was,

I also knew better than to miss the opportunity, even though I didn't know what the opportunity was. I turned to the Rabbi and introduced Ken and myself and told him that we had been to one of their Seders, and then I said that during the night the Lord had *impressed* me to pray for his congregation. He thanked me, we made our salads and I gladly took my seat, thinking, "Okay, God, I did what I was supposed to do; now that's over." To my surprise, the Rabbi and Ken struck up a conversation – a long one – long enough to make me squirm in my seat. I was too far away to hear what was being said. All I knew was that the longer they talked, the more my heart pounded. Finally, Ken came to the table and said, "Guess what … we're going to Israel with them in June." God had made arrangements for us to go to Israel (where I'd always wanted to go) – with *believing Jews*!

Dear friend, God seriously desires unity between Israel and the Church. He hates the man-made division separating the two. He longs to see an unbreakable, unshakable bond, corporately and individually. I was beginning to love the sound of my having Jewish roots.

FOUR

"Return to Bethlehem"
Ruth 1:18-22

Elimelech_____ ♰ Naomi _____ ♰ Mahlon _____ ♰

Chilion _____ ♰ Orpah _____ ♰ Ruth _____ ♰

W e concluded the last chapter with Ruth giving her famous speech about total surrender of self to Naomi. She relinquished all that was familiar and comfortable, and determinedly set her face and her heart toward the Promised Land.

Verse 18. ***When she*** (Naomi) ***saw that she*** (Ruth) ***was stedfastly minded to go with her, then she left speaking unto her.*** When one makes an all-inclusive, lifelong vow to another, calling on God Almighty to rain down judgment if the vow is broken, it's time to take hands off. That's exactly what Naomi does. She knows better than to try and dissuade Ruth from her stand. Ruth has crossed that critical line – she's put her hand to the plow – and the consequences are grave should she ever turn back. It must be clearly understood that this is not a commitment *between* Naomi and Ruth. Naomi has no role in keeping this vow. There are no terms, obligations or requirements she must meet; all responsibility rests with Ruth.

There's a wonderful verse in Genesis (12:3) that Ruth, being a Moabite, probably has never heard before. This was where God made a vow to Abraham. It, too, was one-sided with God setting the terms and being solely responsible for seeing that all conditions were met. In this verse God said to Abraham,

> *"I will bless those who bless you* (Israel)*, and I will curse those who curse you."*

Ruth just set herself up, by her own vow, for one or the other – blessing or cursing. The outcome rests entirely on her shoulders.

Verse 19. ***So they two went until they came to Bethlehem. And it came to pass, when they were come to Bethlehem, that all the city was moved about them, and they said, Is this Naomi?*** Why didn't those in the city just say, "Look, Naomi's come back home?" Why did they question whether or not it really was her? Could they not recognize her? Had those ten years in Moab changed her that much? Or, were they "moved" because she left with three men and came back with one woman – a Moabite? Perhaps, it was because she left a "queen," (since her husband had the kingly name of Elimelech), but, upon her return, the queen was dethroned because there was no king. Possibly, she left Bethlehem a little arrogant, "looking down" on those less fortunate because they *had* to stay behind, "poor things." Why this buzz throughout *all* the city? We can only speculate; we don't know. But, what we do know is that she is definitely different than when she left.

Verse 20. ***And she said unto them, Call me not Naomi, call me Mara: for the Almighty hath dealt very bitterly with me.*** This verse and the next both have to do with her name. In the previous verse they asked, "Is this Naomi?" which seems to have struck a raw nerve with her. But, before we try to expose that nerve, let's look at the new name she's chosen for herself. Mara is the Hebrew word for "bitter." We've seen it before during the wanderings of the Hebrew children. In Exodus 15:22-25 we read:

So Moses brought Israel from the Red sea, and they went out into the wilderness of Shur; and they went three days in the wilderness, and found no water. And when they came to Marah (same Hebrew word), they could not drink of the waters of Marah, for they were bitter: therefore the name of it was called Marah. And the people murmured against Moses, saying, What shall we drink? And he cried unto the Lord; and the Lord shewed him a tree, which when he had cast into the waters, the waters were made sweet: there he made for them a statute and an ordinance, and there he proved them.

There's no question that she undoubtedly feels just like that bitter water in the desert – useless and good for nothing. Her name, Naomi, which means "My Pleasantness" no longer seems appropriate. Therefore, she openly displays her rebellious spirit by choosing for herself a new name. She changes her name to "Bitter."

Verse 21. *I went out full, and the Lord hath brought me home again empty: why then call ye me Naomi, seeing the Lord hath testified against me, and the Almighty hath afflicted me?* She continues with her justification for changing her name. It is as though she sarcastically flaunts her name before God. Why does she so disdain the name Naomi – *His* pleasantness? If you'll look very carefully in these two verses, you'll see to whom the "His" refers. The "His" is Almighty God, and she's blaming *Him* for not allowing her life to reflect the Hebrew meaning of her name. She says, "How can *I* be *His* pleasantness when *He* made my life very bitter? *I* went away full, but *He* brought me back empty and afflicted me and brought misfortune on me. If *I* were really *His* Pleasantness, then *He* would never have done those things to me, so *I'm* changing my name!"

She's angry, embarrassed, indignant, defiant, hurt and she's not holding anything back. She has an audience and she's playing to it.

Who has the privilege of naming someone? It is the one who owns or who has the responsibility, or control, over that person.

Parents, because of their charge over their children, have the privilege and honor of naming them. Children belong to their parents. In addition, sometimes in Scripture we see names changed because of new positions or assignments. God changed Abram to Abraham, Sarai to Sarah, Saul to Paul, signifying their new roles. Nebuchadnezzar, King of Babylon captured Daniel and his three friends, and as a sign of his control over them, changed their names to Belteshazzar, Shadrach, Meshach and Abednego.

Naomi, in changing her name before this crowd of witnesses, exhibits extreme independence and defiance against the One who named her. God gave her that name, and He hasn't changed his mind. "Yet," she says, "I am no longer *His* Pleasantness; I refuse that name; I choose rather to be known as 'Bitter.'" Her rebellious outburst, attitude and arrogance are visible signs of her total lack of submission. The ten years in Moab produced no humility or repentance. She continues in her spiritual famine.

But, the thing that really excites me about this whole Exodus 15 scenario is what happened next to that bitter water and the children of Israel. Thankfully, the story doesn't end with the useless water and Israel unquenched. God told Moses to pick up something plain, common and ordinary – a tree – and throw it in the water. Moses obeyed, and the water became *sweet* – one tree reversed the worthlessness of an entire body of water, giving life to over a million thirsty people. Oh, God's miraculous provisions for the Hebrew children! Incredibly, too, in our story, God picks up a plain, common, ordinary nobody, a nothing, and He thrusts her into the "sea" of Israel. Through this one (Ruth), He will provide sweet nourishment, not only to Naomi, but to all the House of Judah, all Israel and ultimately to the whole world.

Verse 22. *So Naomi returned, and Ruth the Moabitess, her daughter in law, with her, which returned out of the country of Moab: and they came to Bethlehem in the beginning of barley harvest.* This little phrase "the beginning of barley harvest" opens up another whole realm that would easily be missed without some knowledge of Jewish customs and traditions. Do you recall back in the very beginning my telling about calling the grocery and asking how many items they stocked? The answer was an astonishing "30,000 normally and up to 50,000 for major holidays." I knew from my many years of grocery shopping that there were considerably more items found at Christmastime, Thanksgiving and Easter, but I had no idea that the amount nearly doubled. That is exactly what is about to happen in our story. Once we lay this book against its rightful, Jewish backdrop, which must include the Jewish holidays, our events in Ruth seem to *explode* with new meaning and illumination.

In Scripture there were three major holidays when all Jewish males were *required* to go to Jerusalem.[14] The women and children were also allowed to go if their household chores permitted. These three holidays are Passover (*Feast of Unleavened Bread,* or *First Fruits*), Shavuot (*Feast of Weeks, Pentecost*) and Sukkot (*Feast of Tabernacles*). (The outline of all three can be found in the Appendix, Charts 5, 6 and 7.)

Simply stated, **Passover**, with its observance of eating *Unleavened Bread*, is followed on the first day of the week by waving the *First Fruits* offering. This begins a seven-week (50-day) period known as the *Counting of the Omer*, during which grain is harvested. **Shavuot** (SHEH VUH OTE) (*Weeks, Pentecost*) is observed at the end of this 50-day period. At this celebration, the Temple priest waves two loaves of bread from the newly harvested grain. Then follows another period of time (not always a set time), after which comes the third and final holiday known as **Sukkot** (*Ingathering, Tabernacles*). Sukkot is a seven-day celebration for remembering the 40 years of wandering in the wilderness, with a holy assembly on the eighth day.

This little phrase in our verse, "the beginning of barley harvest," signals the first of these three major holidays, Passover. (Shavuot will be covered at Ruth 4:13, and Sukkot at Ruth 4:17.) These three holidays are called major holidays because a pilgrimage is required. Each of the three is linked one to the other without a break.

Most Christians are somewhat familiar with Passover. We know it as the holiday commemorating the quick departure of the Israelites from Egypt. But, what is not generally known is that coinciding with this holiday are two other events: *Feast of Unleavened*

Bread[15] and *First Fruits.*[16] These three are all grouped together under the general term of Passover because they take place at the same time. (The *"Did you Know?"* segment designed to correlate with this chapter is on Passover and gives interesting illustrations.)

At this point in our study, we will look at Passover, the first required trip to Jerusalem, and view it during four biblical time periods: (1) the time of the Exodus; (2) the time of our story (Boaz, Naomi and Ruth); (3) the time of Christ and (4) present-day Judaism.

At the time of the Exodus, the Hebrew children were told to take the blood of a lamb and apply it to their doorposts on the night of **Passover**.[17] In addition, that night and for the next seven days, they were to eat only bread without leaven (yeast). Thus, those particular days are known as the *Feast of Unleavened Bread*. On the Sunday after their hasty departure, the Hebrew children were permanently delivered from Egyptian bondage when the waters of the Red Sea swallowed all of Pharaoh's army. This day, the Sunday after Passover,[18] is known as *First Fruits*. When those Hebrew children walked through the Sea and emerged safely on the other side, they became the *First Fruits* offering to the Lord. It was a fresh beginning, a new start, and there was great anticipation for much more to come. The "Counting of the Omer" began (seven weeks, 50 days), in which the children of Israel were being distanced from their former life, and were learning to follow God and adapt to new leadership (Moses).

During our second period, **Passover at the time of our story** – Boaz, as an observant Jewish man, would have made the required pilgrimage.[19] (The Temple was not yet built in Jerusalem, so he would have gone to the Tabernacle, probably located in Shiloh.)[20] There he would have eaten the Passover meal with family and friends, retelling the Biblical account of the Exodus (just as it is observed today, thousands of years later). That night and for the seven days following, Boaz would have observed the *Feast of Unleavened Bread* by eating nothing containing leaven. He would have remained there through Sunday ("the day after the Sabbath, or the first day of the week," Leviticus 23:11) to present his required *First Fruits* offering (his tithe). A part of this tithe was a sheaf of barley cut from the new crop and taken to the priest to wave before the Lord. Prior to leaving for the celebration, Boaz would have gone into his field and cut this sheaf of barley. The landowners were not allowed in their fields to harvest the barley crop until after they had performed this duty. This first fruits offering, or wave offering, was a time of rejoicing before the Lord for His provision (especially after a ten-year famine), and for the promise of much more to come. After satisfying this requirement, Boaz would have returned home to begin the harvest season during the "Counting of the Omer." It was during this counting period that Ruth went into his fields. This was the time God used in the Exodus story to distance the Hebrew children from their former life, to teach them to follow Him and to adapt to new leadership. Do you think Ruth might have been learning those same lessons, as well?

During **the time of Christ** – we know for certain Jesus and His disciples went to Jerusalem and ate the required **Passover** meal and the *Unleavened Bread* in the upper room. The Passover Lamb was betrayed, crucified, buried and on the Sunday after Passover, was raised the *First Fruits* from the dead – the Ultimate *Wave Offering*. Listen to what Paul says about the Sunday after Passover, *First Fruits*. In I Corinthians 15:20, we read:

> *But now is Christ risen from the dead, and become the firstfruits of them that slept.*

This is the offering thanking God for His Provision and for the promise of much more to come. During the following seven weeks (50 days) of the "Counting of the Omer," Jesus made numerous appearances to His disciples and others, and on the fortieth day, ascended into Heaven. It was during this time that his followers were learning to distance themselves from their former lives, follow God with all their hearts and adapt to new Leadership – the Comforter, the Holy Spirit.

Finally, we look at the observance of **Passover**, *Feast of Unleavened Bread* and *First Fruits* during **present-day Judaism**. Sad to say, there are many voids in this cycle. Passover is a faithfully-kept feast. Jewish families and friends all over the world gather in homes, eating *unleavened bread* and retelling the story of that first Passover night in Egypt. Although this is required to be observed in Jerusalem, there is no Temple standing, so the requirement cannot be met. An interesting aspect of the Passover celebration is that at the meal's conclusion, everyone exuberantly shouts, "Next Year in Jerusalem!" This affirms their desire to obey the pilgrimage command. Also, the wave offering required the Sunday after Passover (*First Fruits*), cannot be performed because there is no Temple. Jewish families observe the "Counting of the Omer" by marking the time on their calendars.

There's an intriguing element about Naomi's and Ruth's homecoming at this particular time. When Naomi and Ruth arrived in Bethlehem, we read, "*...and they said, is this Naomi?*" The interesting word that I want you to see is "they." In Hebrew this word is *plural feminine.* That is extremely significant. Only women were doing the talking. The reason I am so confident that there were no men present is because of a grammatical rule our Hebrew teacher drilled in us. She said, "If in a room of 5,000 people, there were 4,999 women and only one man, the gender for *they*, referring to the people in that room, would be masculine." She said this rule applies *every* time and in *every* situation, no exception. Therefore, we have to conclude that there were no men present when Naomi gave her defiant little speech changing her name.

I want you to look at one possibility as to why there were no men present. I personally believe they were not there because Naomi planned it that way. She knew exactly when the men would leave for Passover, and she knew exactly when they would return. Being the shrewd, intelligent wife of someone like Elimelech, Naomi knew the exact window of opportunity available for her to make her entrance into town and not have to face the men. The women would be painful enough, but she could "show off" a little in front of them, but never in front of the men. How else could all these women have had such liberty to leave their chores and gather around, humoring Naomi while she's wallowing in her self pity and defiantly changing her name? Another reason why I have come to this conclusion is because I am a woman, and that's exactly what I would do. If I were in the same situation, you can be sure I would sneak home when I could spout off and make a scene and not have to worry about being reprimanded for it.

Also, don't forget that she has Ruth by her side now. Does she really want Ruth to see her coming home amid raised eyebrows, whispers and condescending looks, or would she rather take command of the situation and act like she's still in control? She would certainly feel better about herself if she could be the one calling the shots. She assuredly would not want to be humiliated in front of Ruth. This was the perfect time for her homecoming, and Bethlehem was where she belonged.

She may have planned her arrival home to suit herself, but she could never out-plan God. Indeed it was the perfect time to come home. God had made everything ready for "*their* homecoming."

FIVE

"Boaz Meets Ruth"
Ruth 2:1-10

Elimelech_____ ⚦ Naomi _____ ⚦ Mahlon _____ ⚦

Chilion _____ ⚦ Orpah _____ ⚦ Ruth _____ ⚦

Verse 1. *And Naomi had a kinsman of her husband's, a mighty man of wealth, of the family of Elimelech; and his name was Boaz.* In studying Ruth carefully, I found the placement of this verse very intriguing. Nothing has been mentioned about Boaz up to this point. Ruth has not yet gone into the fields, or even expressed a desire to go, so why, at this particular juncture, would we have an introduction to Boaz? There may be many reasons, but my personal belief is that this verse is in response to the performance just given by Naomi at the end of chapter one. There she proclaimed that there was no hope left for her, and to prove it, she was changing her name to "Bitter." It is as though the Author of the Book can't hold back the good news another moment. Long before Naomi left with Elimelech to go to Moab, long before their two sons, long before Orpah and Ruth came into this family, there was a mighty man of wealth, a man named Boaz. He is not only wealthy enough for Naomi, but he's wealthy enough for Gentile Ruth, too. I believe this verse is suspended high between Heaven and earth

55

anxiously awaiting the return of "empty" Naomi and her "misfit" Moabitess daughter-in-law, Ruth. This verse holds the answers to their every problem and completely dispels all of Naomi's false claims. Boaz can "refill" and "sweeten" disgruntled Naomi, and can also give position to the outsider Ruth. Between these two, he is the perfect bond who not only embraces the vow Ruth made to Naomi, but will restore Naomi's joy by enabling Ruth to keep her vow. He is *exceeding abundantly above all that we* (or either of them) *could ever ask or think* (Ephesians 3:20).

As stated previously, commentators view Boaz as a type of Christ. I believe we will discover as we progress through this study that, indeed, the role of Boaz lines up, without question, to that of Jesus.

Let's see if this opening verse about Boaz could also describe Jesus. Notice first that we are told Boaz was a *kinsman* of Elimelech's. The Hebrew meaning here for the word "kinsman" is phenomenal! It is the word "yada" and means "to know" in the broadest sense. It is all encompassing. It is knowledge not only of the head and heart, but intimate knowledge as well. It is the term used when a husband and wife become one. (Note this is not talking about the relationship between Elimelech and Naomi, but the relationship between Elimelech and Boaz.) The word "kinsman" is used many times in the Book of Ruth, but only in this verse is it this particular Hebrew word. The relationship between Elimelech and Boaz is as though the two were one.

In further describing Boaz, the writer uses the word "mighty," which translates, "warrior, champion, chief, a valiant man." He's also said to be a "man of wealth." This phrase translates he's a "force" – militarily, through resources, virtue or strength. The Boaz in our story, this kinsman of Elimelech, is a mighty warrior and a champion; he's rich; he's a force not only militarily, but also in resources and strength. Could all these terms also apply to Boaz's allegorical role? Isn't Jesus the Mightiest of the mighty, the Wealthiest of the wealthy and the Force behind every other force? Is there any wonder the writer could wait no longer to introduce the true Hero in our story?

Verse 2. ***And Ruth the Moabitess said unto Naomi, Let me
now go to the field, and glean ears of corn after him in whose
sight I shall find grace. And she said unto her, Go, my daughter.***
The barley harvest has begun. The fields are certainly teeming with
activity after ten years of famine. It must be very exciting to see the
people of Bethlehem going about their business with renewed hope
and enthusiasm.

Ruth asks Naomi for permission to go into the fields. Why
would anyone come up with such a plan as to go to the fields and
pick up leftover grain? How does she know this is allowed? And,
how does she know she wouldn't get kicked out of the fields? The
truth is she probably could get kicked out of some fields, but she's
willing to take the chance. And, somehow she must have heard
about the God of Israel's "welfare program." (We didn't invent the
welfare program; God did. It's found in Leviticus 23:22.)

> *And when ye reap the harvest of your land, thou
> shalt not make clean riddance of the corners of thy
> field when thou reapest, neither shalt thou gather
> any gleaning of thy harvest: thou shalt leave them
> unto the poor, and to the stranger: I am the Lord
> your God.*

God's program doesn't take away our incentive to work. The
landowner was commanded by God not to reap to the very edges or
to go back over the crop a second time. These corners and drop-
pings were for the poor, the widows, the strangers and the aliens.
The amount the landowner was instructed to leave behind could
have been as much as 20 – 30 percent of his crop. We have a very
benevolent Provider.

At harvest time the reapers would cut the ripened grain with
wooden sickles. Then binders would follow tying the stalks into
bundles called sheaves. After that, the gleaners were allowed in the
fields to gather stalks missed by the binders. These gleaners were
the widows, the orphans and the strangers. They would tie up these
missed stalks in the folds of their long veils.[21]

Ruth asks permission of Naomi to go into the fields, which she grants by saying, "Go, my daughter." She then goes out, by faith, seeking that field in which she would be extended grace (favor).

(The King James Version reads that she went out to glean "ears of corn." Holman Bible Dictionary states that corn is "a general term used by the translators of the KJV for any grain."[22] In Hebrew this verse reads, "let me pick up among the grains.")

Verse 3. *And she went, and came, and gleaned in the field after the reapers: and her hap* (she just happened) *was to light on a part of the field belonging unto Boaz, who was of the kindred of Elimelech.* Her venture "just happened" to land her in the field of Boaz. Why was she drawn to this particular field? Had she passed up others? Was this the first? Did his crop seem more abundant than the others? Were there more gleaners in his field among whom she could hopefully disguise herself? We have no idea the answer to these questions. But, this we do know:

> *"...all things work together for good to them that love God, to them who are the called according to His purpose* (Romans 8:28)."

One day I asked my Daddy, concerning this verse, "Does 'all things' mean 'all things?'" He said, "Well, of course!" Then I said, "Daddy, if I *deliberately* sin, is that an 'all things?'" He had to ponder that a minute, and then said, "Yes, even deliberate sins have to be an 'all things.'" Our great God is amazing! He loves Naomi and Ruth; they are most assuredly called according to His purpose. This "fortunate happenstance" of being in Boaz's field had nothing to do with fortune, and it didn't just happen. It was God's eternal design. He deliberately placed Ruth in that field. She was exactly where she was supposed to be.

Verse 4. *And, behold, Boaz came from Bethlehem, and said unto the reapers, The Lord be with you. And they answered him, The Lord bless thee.* How would you like to be a beggar and find yourself in this kind of environment? Little Ruth must be cautiously taking in everything being said and done around her. She may never have done this type work before, and for sure we know she hasn't in Israel. She was probably being extra cautious so as not to offend or make a wrong move. But, I'm sure no scene ever played out like this in Moab – field hands being blessed by the owner! "The Lord be with you," he says. What more can any of us ask than to have the very presence of the Lord with us? What an amazing salutation! And, in response to his greeting, they return a blessing. This is as it should be. The True Landowner always deserves our blessing.

Verse 5. ***Then said Boaz unto his servant that was set over the reapers, Whose damsel is this?*** This servant, or foreman, is responsible for everything that takes place in Boaz's field. The reapers and binders are paid workers, and it is his job to oversee them and their work. In addition, the gleaners (the "beggars") are equally his charge. He must see to it that they keep their distance from the reapers and binders to make sure the harvest progresses speedily and without incident.

Why does Ruth stand out so? Is Bethlehem such a small place that everybody knows everybody else? Is it because she is visibly a foreigner? Is it because under these circumstances it is not common to see a widow so young? Whatever the reason, her presence is noticed by Boaz. He asks the one in charge of his field, "Whose damsel is this?" Isn't that a strange question? We would say, "Who is that person?" but never "*Whose* is that person?" This further illustrates what we said in chapter one about the necessity for a woman to have male covering. Boaz asks, "Whose property is she?" The sad truth is she doesn't belong to anyone anymore. She is minus her male covering. That's why she is in this predicament.

Verses 6 and 7. ***And the servant that was set over the reapers answered and said, It is the Moabitish damsel that came back with Naomi out of the country of Moab: And she said, I pray you, let me glean and gather after the reapers among the sheaves: so she came, and hath continued even from the morning until now, that she tarried a little in the house.*** The servant had no answer for the question as to "whose" she was, but rather, he told Boaz of her heritage. You will recall in chapter one how Naomi gave her academy award performance before a group of women. No doubt, by now everybody in town knows the story of Naomi coming home with no husband or sons, just this Moabite daughter-in-law. We are told the whole town was astir. This is probably the juiciest piece of gossip Bethlehem has heard in a long time. The foreman responds, "She's that Moabitess damsel who came back with Naomi from Moab." The meaning of the Hebrew word used here to describe Ruth (damsel) is that of a very young female in the age range of infancy to adolescence.

The foreman continues supplying information to Boaz about what he knows of Ruth. He says she has manners and respects authority because she asked permission to glean in the field. He further says, "She arrived at morning time and worked steadily from then until now, taking only a short rest in the house (or shelter)." We know this is shortly after Passover, about mid-April, and as their weather is similar to ours here in the Mid-South, it was probably not yet extremely hot. However, let's not forget that she just recently made an approximate 40-mile journey from Moab. (See Map in the Appendix.) This journey would not only have included the travel, but the packing and preparation for the trip, the agony of leaving family and friends behind forever, and then the unpacking upon arrival in Bethlehem. It is likely she was one weary, tired young girl. Her short rest was probably not a luxury but a necessity.

Verse 8. ***Then said Boaz unto Ruth, Hearest thou not, my daughter? Go not to glean in another field, neither go from hence, but abide here fast by my maidens:*** Something truly amazing in this verse immediately jumps off the page. He calls her "my daughter." Why, that's the same thing Naomi's been calling her (1:11; 1:12; 1:13; 2:2). Isn't that an odd way for Boaz to address Ruth? Let's stop here for just a minute and ponder this. Boaz is obviously a devout, observant Jewish man of prominence, an older man because he's a contemporary of Elimelech's. Ruth is quite young, a widow, probably attractive and with a little mystique about her since she's from another country. If this older man entertains thoughts of romance, do you think he would ever address her as his "daughter*?"* *Or, should such a greeting alert the reader to other, more obvious intentions*?

Also, why would Boaz give her a string of do's and don'ts? This sounds more like *fatherly* advice, rather than romantic interest. Did he realize she would go back and tell Naomi all he said, including his calling her "his daughter?" We'll pursue this line of thinking a little later, but for now let's take a look at this "fatherly" advice he gives.

Verse 9. *Let thine eyes be on the field that they do reap, and go thou after them: have I not charged the young men that they shall not touch thee? And when thou art athirst, go unto the vessels and drink of that which the young men have drawn.* In this verse and the previous one, Boaz gives Ruth seven specific instructions. They are:

(1) "Hearest thou," that is, "listen to me." If she's not paying attention, then all his words are for naught.

(2) "Don't go and glean in another field." He has absolute, total and complete authority over this field. It belongs to him. He is the master, and on this turf all obey his voice. But, if she were to go into another field, she would be placing herself outside his realm of authority. He couldn't help her there.

(3) "Neither go from hence" – don't go away from this place. This is the place of safety; this is the place of provision. It is here and only here that she will find the "filling" for her *empty* mother-in-law (1:21) and a home and a people for herself (2:5-6).

(4) "Abide here fast by my maidens." These maidens, or young servant girls, are indebted to Boaz. He is their master. They know his manner and his expectations. They can guide and instruct her.

(5) "Let thine eyes be on the field that they do reap." This actually translates, "eyes of you in the field." Don't let your eyes wander, or allow other fields to tempt you. Don't lose focus; keep your eyes fixed *in* this field.

(6) "Go thou after them," or "follow behind my servant girls." They would be a buffer between Ruth and the men, somewhat of a wall of protection. After this particular instruction, he adds an interesting remark. He says, "Have I not charged the young men that they shall not touch thee?" A Moabite girl would almost certainly have been a target for abuse. Laborers could be crude, not just

verbally, but physically. The reapers would shout at the gleaners if they got too close, and how much more so if the gleaner were a foreigner? She would have been at great risk for being heckled and even molested. But, if she follows *after* his girls, as he instructs, she's assured safety. Incidentally, the word "touch" here means "to lay a hand on, to rape, or to strike." Women are the weaker vessel; we are keenly aware of our vulnerability. We can be certain Ruth knew her vulnerability as a young widow in a foreign country among the "enemy" nation?

(7) Finally, he says, "When thou art athirst, go unto the vessels and drink of that which the young men have drawn." These are the same young men who, if she were not shielded, could lay a hand on her, rape her, or strike her. Rather than the abuse they might have desired to inflict, their instructions were to draw water to satisfy her thirst. The same ones who might wish to harm her are the very ones instructed to bring water to refresh her. The Psalmist says (Psalm 23:5a):

Thou preparest a table before me in the presence of mine enemies.

Looking back over these seven directives of Boaz (a picture of Jesus) – could they apply to us today (the Church) "spiritually?" "Listen to me – don't go in another field – don't go away – stay with my servants – keep your eyes in the field – follow behind those who were there before you – and, when you're thirsty, it's available." If that comforts us today, just imagine how comforting it was for that young Moabite girl in the middle of a strange, foreign land on that day.

Verse 10. *Then she fell on her face, and bowed herself to the ground, and said unto him, Why have I found grace in thine eyes, that thou shouldest take knowledge of me, seeing I am a stranger?* How could she respond in any other manner? She bows with her face to the ground in total humility. The definition for bowed in this verse means to pay homage to royalty. (Isn't that interesting?) "What an appropriate response, Ruth!" And, yet, she has no idea of the true identity of this man.

What was there about *her*—this young Moabite woman – that caused him to act so *irrationally*? Why did she find such favor in his sight? Why did he notice her, a foreigner? Wasn't she already in his field gathering grain she hadn't sown, watered, tended or cut – wasn't that kindness enough? What was there that made him offer his field, protection and provision? Why did he tell his men not to touch her? Why did he care about this "Moabitess?"

With her limited understanding, she cannot comprehend such kindness and favor. There may have been a dozen others gleaning in his field that day. What made her stand out? Then there's the mystery of him calling her, "my daughter." Was that for her benefit, *or possibly someone else's*? How puzzling it must have been to hear him call her the same thing as her dear mother-in-law.

What she didn't understand is something probably everybody else in the field did. They knew Naomi was the wife of his beloved relative, Elimelech; they knew Boaz was a kinsman-redeemer; and they knew how solemnly Boaz took familial obligations.

SIX

"Boaz Favors Ruth in His Field"
Ruth 2:11-23

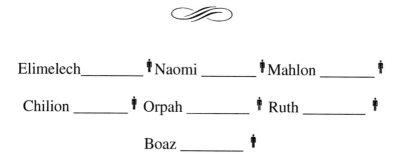

Elimelech_____ Naomi _____ Mahlon _____

Chilion _____ Orpah _____ Ruth _____

Boaz _____

Chapter five ended with Ruth bowing her face to the ground in complete bewilderment at the favor shown her by Boaz, and then asking him (verse 10), *"Why have I found grace in thine eyes, that thou shouldest take knowledge of me, seeing I am a stranger?"*

Verse 11. ***And Boaz answered and said unto her, It hath fully been shewed me, all that thou hast done unto thy mother in law since the death of thine husband: and how thou hast left thy father and thy mother, and the land of thy nativity, and art come unto a people which thou knewest not heretofore.*** The reason for his immense favor toward her is because of what she's done for Naomi. Why would that so impress him? Why does he care? What does her relationship with Naomi have to do with him?

He also mentions her being a widow. This was likely a painful thing for him to say, and probably equally as painful for her to hear.

Yet, it was necessary for him to make this statement. You see, the death of her husband meant that she was a free woman. When Mahlon (her husband) died, she was released from any commitment she had to this family. Boaz says the reason for his grace to her is because she chose her mother-in-law over her own mother, father, brothers, sisters, gods, even the land of her birth when she didn't have to. He says his grace toward her is because she chose Naomi and the Land of Israel over what was comfortable and familiar. But, still, she has to wonder, "What does all of this have to do with him?" And, what about those words, "my daughter?" Is there any explanation? Yes, he answered the questions she posed in verse 10, but his answers only seem to generate more questions. "Who is this man?"

In the very first verse of the second chapter where the writer of the Book of Ruth couldn't wait any longer to introduce Boaz, we discussed the close relationship between Elimelech and Boaz. When you truly love someone (as Boaz did Elimelech), you love, unconditionally, the ones they love. Boaz loved Naomi because of "whose" she was – she was the beloved of Elimelech. Boaz had utmost respect for Elimelech's choice. The first reason Boaz lists as to why he was showing unmerited favor to Ruth was because of her "unconditional" love for the wife of his kinsman, Elimelech.

Verse 12. ***The Lord recompense thy work, and a full reward be given thee of the Lord God of Israel, under whose wings thou art come to trust.*** He continues his dialog with young Ruth who must be trying desperately to comprehend the situation. Do you ever have those times when suddenly you're overwhelmed with the vastness of God's grace to you, and feel the incredulity at Him choosing you? That's probably the same way young Ruth is feeling about now. With each additional word that comes from his mouth, she has to cry deep within herself, "Why me?"

Here in verse 12, he speaks an amazing blessing over her. This verse in the NIV reads,

> *May the Lord repay you for what you have done. May you be richly rewarded by the Lord, the God of Israel, under whose wings you have come to take refuge.*

In verse 11, he explained why he was showing favor toward her (because she renounced her past and embraced Naomi and the people of Israel). Yet, as if his personal favor weren't enough, he continues by asking the Lord, the God of Israel, to "repay" her. Is Israel's God really able to "repay" *her*? She's lost her husband, the possibility of children, her mother, father, siblings, aunts, uncles, cousins, friends, the land of her birth, her gods – she gave it all up – everything! Can the God of Boaz really repay such losses? When you repay something, doesn't that mean you get it *all* back?

But, Boaz doesn't stop there, he continues by asking his God not only to repay her, but to give her a "full reward." Reward means compensation, a profit. There are no gods like that in Moab. For her to be "repaid" and then on top of that to be "rewarded" is far beyond anything to which this Moabitess is accustomed.

If you should have to give up absolutely everything, what would you like in return as repayment? Probably, "I want it all back." And, if you were offered rewards on top of that, what would you ask for? Would it be something like, "I want it all back, but better!" She's a pauper, a charity case, a "nobody" in this land, clinging to another pauper/charity case. Naomi has already told her there's no future for either of them. How can someone in such desperate circumstances be repaid and richly rewarded? Can't this man see she is in his field picking up leftovers just so there will be food on the table? Who can comprehend the mysterious words pouring from this stranger's lips?

The last thing he says in this verse speaks of her new lodging place. He says she is "under the wings of the God of Israel in Who she's come to trust." Had she realized her choice of Israel over Moab meant that her new home would be under the wings of this new God – the God in Who she now "trusts?" How does he know she trusts in Israel's God? Could her denouncement of her former life mean anything else? The word "trust" means "to flee for protection, to have hope or to make refuge." It would appear that her new home is more like a fortress. What an incredible place to live. She's under the wings of the God of Abraham, Isaac and Jacob, wings of certain protection, of hope and refuge.

Just a side note to you, dear reader: whenever God gives a

person a burden about a particular matter, often He will use that person to champion the cause, to fight the fight, to right the wrong. If you find yourself "inordinately" praying and concerned over a certain matter, don't be surprised if some where down the line you are the one God uses to fight His fight. Here in our story, will Boaz be the one to see that Ruth is "repaid" and receives those "full rewards?" Will he champion this cause?

This book is written because God uniquely spoke to me about Ruth, but my interest in Jewish/Christian relations actually began long before my "Ruth" encounter. It goes back nearly 30 years. Ken and I have three sons, and our first was hyperactive. My heart goes out to all "special" children. They are bright, funny, lovable, entertaining, but at times very difficult to control. We knew early on he was unique and needed a structured environment, so we put him in a Christian school. Every day was challenging. I was making all his food from scratch and not giving him sugar, additives or artificial colorings, but nothing really made an impact. It seemed we were having parent-teacher conferences weekly, and I dreaded hearing the phone ring. It was such an overwhelming time in our lives. We were attacked on every hand for our "poor parenting." The school's principal and some teachers were callous (even with the title of a "Christian" school). Many in our own family were judgmental and crude, and only a few friends embraced our child with unconditional love.

One evening after baths, our second son decided to put hair spray on his hair. (He was about 6 and the hyper one about 8.) Our 6-year old had seen us do it many times, and thought, "Why not?" Afterwards, the two boys went down for the night in the same room with the door closed. The next morning I was in the kitchen making breakfast, and our oldest son crawled from their room to the kitchen on his belly (like a soldier), looked up at me and screamed, "Good morning, Mom!" I could not believe my eyes. I thought, "What has happened?" (It was only later I realized the hairspray, the closed room, and the fumes made his sensitive system go haywire.) I continued the normal routine, trying to calm him, and sent him off to school, knowing I would soon get a call. After everyone was gone, I dropped to my knees in front of our couch and cried out to the Lord in tears and desperation and said, "God, I have done everything humanly possible. There's nothing left in me. If you don't help, then there is no help." Instantly, God spoke in my Spirit and said, "Now do you see how I feel with my Israel?" That was like a jolt that shot straight through me. I immediately went from my knees to a sitting position, and thought, "What just happened?" I had never experienced anything like that before. Then I began thinking about what I had prayed and what I heard. It was true that almost no one liked our son – family, most friends, even "Christians." Did God feel the same way about Israel? What about her "family" (Arabs)? And, what about her "friends?" (Most of them only give lip service.) And, what about "Christians?" (Check out the track record for the Church regarding Israel. It's appalling.) This son was our firstborn, just as Israel is God's (Exodus 4:22). And, as our parenting was always being called into question, I wondered if the same were true for God toward His firstborn?

That son is my heartbeat, as are both our other sons. If God felt anything at all like I was feeling with my firstborn, then my heart broke for His pain, too. And, that was exactly what He wanted from me. He wanted my heart to break and begin beating for Israel. At that moment, I told the Lord that in a very small way I understood, and I was going to pray for His Israel every day for the rest of my life. That was a long time ago, and I've tried to be faithful to my word.

I told you all of this to illustrate the point … when someone has compassion and concern for another (as Boaz did Ruth), it rarely stops there. God frequently draws that person into personal involvement. I had no intention of ever being any more involved with Israel than honoring my commitment to pray daily for her. I never dreamed or expected it to go any further than that.

Verse 13. ***Then she*** (Ruth) ***said, Let me find favour in thy sight, my lord; for that thou hast comforted me, and for that thou hast spoken friendly unto thine handmaid, though I be not like unto one of thine handmaidens.*** What if on that particular day everybody had been snubbing Ruth? What if all day long she was made to feel like filthy Moabite scum in refined, elite Israel? Indeed, his words must have been like a soothing balm.

She tells him she wants to continue finding favor in his eyes, and then she tells him that she knows her place. She refers to herself as his handmaid, or servant, and says that she's beneath any of his other servant girls. These servant girls were quite possibly female slaves, yet she has placed herself below that level. Ruth, in her response, displays total humility.

Verse 14. *And Boaz said unto her, At mealtime come thou hither, and eat of the bread, and dip thy morsel in the vinegar. And she sat beside the reapers: and he reached her parched corn, and she did eat, and was sufficed, and left.* Ruth asked in the previous verse that she continue finding favor in his eyes, and she certainly seems to have found it in this verse. What a happy time this must have been after ten years of famine. Even though the work is back breaking, there is joy in having the work to do. It's mealtime, and they gather around for bread and dipping sauce, plus munching on roasted grain (translated parched corn). Food after work is always enjoyable; how much more so food after famine? Boaz personally invites Ruth to come and join him and his workers. She is served the same food as the master of the field, the foreman, the paid workers, and his servant girls. It may have been almost like a party atmosphere – and she's invited! (Just a reminder … at this time she doesn't know of the relationship between Boaz and Elimelech.)

He passes her grain. She eats what she wants and has leftovers. The King James translation says, "she was sufficed, and left," but the Hebrew renders, "she was filled and she had left over." At the table of Boaz, there's more than enough. She finishes eating and ties her leftover grain in her clothes. She has a gift for someone special!

Was she sitting there enjoying the lively conversation, daring not to join in, yet longing for Naomi to be there to witness this? She had to have been thinking, "Oh, Naomi, you just wouldn't believe this day; I wish you were here. You would be right in the middle." It is wonderful to dine with the Master, to be included, knowing you're not worthy and not even on the same level as all the others present. Regardless of how grateful it might make us feel (like

Ruth), how painful the reality that there are those we love dearly who never make it to the fellowship table.

Verse 15. ***And when she was risen up to glean, Boaz commanded his young men, saying, Let her glean even among the sheaves, and reproach her not:*** In verse 9 Boaz told the men not to touch her, not to strike or rape her, then after the meal he gives further orders concerning her welfare. These are not suggestions; they are commands. He tells his men that even if she takes the cut grain or the grain they've tied in bundles, she is not to be embarrassed. This word "reproach" translates, "wound, taunt, insult, put to shame or make blush." The gleaners know their boundary – they are to gather only what is dropped, or missed, after the grain is tied into bundles. But, here Boaz gives Ruth freedom to gather even what his paid laborers have freshly cut and/or what has been tied into bundles. Before she ever makes a mistake – before doing anything wrong – she's given complete immunity! No matter what blunders she makes – he says, "She's innocent." She is not to be reprimanded in any way or for any reason. *They* can be reprimanded if they don't obey his orders, but not Ruth. No matter what transgression, she is completely exonerated. (Don't you love the thought of being declared innocent on the front end of all offences?)

Verse 16. ***And let fall also some of the handfuls of purpose for her, and leave them, that she may glean them, and rebuke her not.*** "Oh, and by-the-way," Boaz says, "One more thing, fellows, go ahead and pull out some of your stalks from your bundles and drop them for her 'accidentally/on purpose.'" This last statement may have made them wonder if he had gone over the edge. He's paying them to cut, pick up and bundle the grain, and now he wants them to pull it out and leave it for this *Moabite* girl – on purpose? Are they thinking he's lost his mind, or lapsed into his second childhood, or been overcome by a pretty face? They couldn't touch her or reprimand her in *any way*, and now they have to continue with their bundling and tying, all the while pulling some out *intentionally* for her. Either he has been smitten romantically, or else he has a serious allegiance somewhere … an allegiance beyond comprehension.

Verse 17. *So she gleaned in the field until even, and beat out that she had gleaned: and it was about an ephah of barley.* She gleaned from morning (which can be as early as dawn or daybreak) until evening (which is dusk or sundown). She was possibly in the field for 12 hours, but after her encounter with Boaz, the time must have flown by with her replaying all the unbelievable scenes over and over in her head.

She threshed the barley, which means she separated the grain from the straw. In the evening there were cool breezes that would come in off the Mediterranean Sea. The stalks of barley would be beaten and then tossed into the air. The breezes would blow the straw outer covering away, and the heavy grain would fall to the ground. She had a very impressive first day's yield. An ephah is about 3/5th of a bushel, or about 22 liters. To put it in lay terms, that's 11 two-liter drink bottles! Has the God of Israel already begun to "repay" and "richly reward" as Boaz had asked?

In one of the teaching sessions I did on Ruth, there was a farmer from Arkansas in the class. He raised grain and shared with us that a bushel of grain weighs 60 pounds. Ruth did quite well her first day; she took home about 36 pounds of barley.

Verse 18. *And she took it up, and went into the city: and her mother in law saw what she had gleaned: and she brought forth, and gave to her that she had reserved after she was sufficed.* Just imagine young Ruth floating on air going home, probably oblivious to the walk or her heavy load. She must certainly be dirty from head to toe, her clothes caked with dust and her hair matted from perspiration, but she's one happy Moabite girl in the land of Israel. She arrives and proudly displays for Naomi "her harvest." Then, with great pride she takes out her little surprise package she's saved for Naomi that she had tucked away at lunchtime.

Verse 19. *And her mother in law said unto her, Where hast thou gleaned to day? And where wroughtest thou? Blessed be he that did take knowledge of thee. And she shewed her mother in law with whom she had wrought, and said, The man's name with whom I wrought to day is Boaz.* Had Naomi worried about Ruth all day, and as the sun began to set, was she concerned that something might have happened to her? Those thoughts probably did run through her head. She knew how cruel hired laborers could be. Then to have Ruth arrive with smiles, food and an unbelievable amount of barley – how astonished Naomi must have been! There had to have been many questions. "Where did you glean; are you okay; were you mistreated?" But, before these could be answered, Naomi blesses the benevolent landowner that took notice of Ruth. Before hearing his name, she blesses him. It was hard to contain eager Ruth with all her youthful enthusiasm – then Naomi heard her say, "His name is Boaz."

When we see God's hand obviously at work in our lives, do we exude excitement? Are we so overjoyed that people can't help but ask, "Tell me what's going on in your life. What is *His* name?" Ruth in her simple and uncluttered manner shared with Naomi her experience of being in the field of Boaz. It was so natural to tell the story, and it ought to be just as simple, uncluttered and natural for us today when those same questions are asked of us.

Verse 20. ***And Naomi said unto her daughter in law, Blessed be he of the Lord, who hath not left off his kindness to the living and to the dead. And Naomi said unto her, The man is near of kin unto us, one of our next kinsmen.*** In the previous verse Ruth shared all she knew about Boaz from her first-hand experience. She had physically been in his field ... eaten with him ... listened to him ... looked into his eyes ... taken in all of his gentle manner-isms, and from her personal experience, she told Naomi about the incredible, generous, gentleman Boaz.

Naomi asks the Lord to bless him, and then she tells Ruth what she herself knows about Boaz – a most unusual thing. "He has not stopped showing his kindness to the living and the *dead*." How "on earth" do you show kindness to a dead person? I understand being kind to a living person – but to a dead person? Boaz had a very unique relationship with Elimelech. It is to this dear relative, because of his utmost love, respect and servitude to him, that Boaz shares freely with Naomi and Ruth. Though Elimelech is no longer present, Boaz continues showing his love for him by loving what was his.

However, I think the real understanding of this phrase is found in the allegorical realm. In that arena Naomi is a picture of Israel. In Ezekiel 37, the prophet likens her to the valley of dry – *dead* – bones, and says she will live again! But, she's not the only one who goes from death to life. What about the Church (Gentile believers), portrayed by Ruth? In Ephesians 2:1, Paul tells us that God has quickened (made alive) those of us who were *dead* in trespasses and sins. We, too, were once dead, and in that hopeless, helpless existence – but, Jesus made a way where there seemed to be no way. What was said of Boaz can also be said of Jesus, "He's good to the living and the *dead*."

Naomi continues, "He is near of kin unto us, one of our next kinsmen." Earlier in this study of Ruth we touched briefly on the kinsman-redeemer role. Here we'll look at it a little more in depth, through illustration.

God ordained that family members were to redeem when there was a gap in the lineage, in order to preserve the deceased's name and to keep the property within the family. This was apparently a very serious matter with God, as seen through the line of Judah. (Turn in the Appendix to Chart #4, Judah/Tamar. The full account of this story is found in Genesis 38, and will be covered more fully in a later chapter.) Judah had three sons by a Canaanite (Gentile) wife before her death. God took the first son, Er, because he was wicked. Judah then gave Er's wife, Tamar, to his second son, Onan. Onan wasn't thrilled with this arrangement, so every time they had sexual intercourse, he conveniently removed himself at the strategic moment so as not to produce offspring for his brother. This greatly displeased God, so He took the second son, as well. Judah promised Tamar his third son when he became of age. From this we see the intent and purpose of the kinsman-redeemer role and how seriously God views it.

Also, there's another interesting phrase in this verse that says, "He's near of kin to *us,* one of *our* next (or close) kinsmen." How was Boaz kin to *Ruth*; how could he have been a kinsman of *hers*? Ruth was in Bethlehem because she chose to be, not because she belonged. Did Naomi really view Boaz as a relative of Ruth's, or did she throw out this little phrase because the wheels were already beginning to turn as to how she might change their "impossible" situation?

Verse 21. ***And Ruth the Moabitess said, He said unto me also, Thou shalt keep fast by my young men, until they have ended all my harvest.*** What was said in the previous verse about Boaz being *their* kinsman-redeemer might possibly have gone right over Ruth's head. "It has nothing to do with me," she may have thought. So, she continues with her lively conversation about Boaz. She tells Naomi he wants her to stay in his field with his workers until all the grain is harvested. Boaz knows if she stays in his field, he can protect her and continue to provide for both Naomi and Ruth. (Harvest will take 50 days, which time is known as the "Counting of the Omer." Barley matures first and then wheat immediately thereafter. Barley is the grain of commoners and animals; wheat is the more desirable of the two.)

Verse 22. ***And Naomi said unto Ruth her daughter in law, It is good, my daughter, that thou go out with his maidens, that they meet thee not in any other field.*** Let me tell you a tragic but true story of a woman who didn't listen and who wandered into "another field." One day on my husband's lunch hour, he was driving down a seven-lane parkway in our city, which has a speed limit of 45. He was in the far right lane when suddenly, without warning an older woman walked directly into the side of his moving vehicle. She had managed to cross six of the seven lanes. This woman was from another country and was in America visiting family. She wanted to go to a local church to pray like she was used to doing in her country. In that country, churches are always open, and pedestrians always have the right-of-way – on all streets, at all times and all places. She thought nothing of crossing in the middle of this major thoroughfare, feeling confident the traffic would stop for her. How tragic, though, that the laws and regulations of our country are so vastly different from hers. She had been told by her family not to cross the street, but she didn't listen, and it cost her life. Her motives were pure and innocent, but her understanding was "foreign." Both Boaz and Naomi tell Ruth to stay in his fields. They know the dangers.

Verse 23. *So she kept fast by the maidens of Boaz to glean unto the end of barley harvest and of wheat harvest; and dwelt with her mother in law.* Ruth obeyed. She stayed close to his maidens throughout the harvest, while, of course, living with Naomi. This word "dwelt" means to abide, to continue to dwell. Certainly, Ruth continued to live with Naomi; we can't imagine her doing otherwise. We would be so disappointed with anything less. How extremely important for **everyone** that this three-fold union (Boaz, Naomi and Ruth) not be broken! Each of their roles is inextricably woven into the other two, and each is dependent one on the other.

A while back my parents were visiting for the weekend. On that particular Saturday morning, my mother and I noticed a garage sale across the street from our house, and she wanted to go over after breakfast. The family in that house at the time was Taiwanese. I immediately headed for the kitchen gadgets and Mother for the books. Soon, she excitedly came over to me, and with a stunned look on her face and waving a little pamphlet in the air said, "Do you want this?" One look at it and I said, "Absolutely!"

This pamphlet entitled, "Judaism and Christianity," was authored by an orthodox Jew and was published for B'nai B'rith's youth studies – just my level. Previously, we cited works from Messianic Jews and from a Gentile Christian attesting to the church having Jewish roots. Incredibly, that's exactly what this pamphlet taught, too. Here is a short excerpt:

> Christianity arose in Palestine a little less than two thousand years ago ... a movement by Jews, of Jews and for Jews. ... by 150 A.D. it had become an independent religion. ... the new movement changed from being a movement of, by and for Jews (to) a movement of Gentiles, by Gentiles and for Gentiles. ... What had begun as a movement within Judaism was now a separate movement outside it. ... At first Christianity was a movement of Jews which added to its normal Judaism some beliefs about Jesus without subtracting anything. ... Palestinian Jewish Christianity probably observed the Torah. It added

concepts about the Messiahship of Jesus, but probably did not discard any part of contemporary Jewish practice. ... Christianity is an offspring of Judaism from which it took its ethics. ... the Judeo-Christian tradition is a description of a long and ancient heritage which was once a unit, but in our day has survived in several varieties. ... We recognize Christianity as a kindred religion, descended from Judaism. With their heritage related to ours, we have an acute awareness of the high lineage of both Judaism and Christianity.[23]

If the Book of Ruth is indeed an allegory, then what are we to conclude as to the importance of the three-fold relationship between Boaz, Naomi and Ruth (Jesus, Israel and the Church – true believers)? Is there relevance in that realm the one for the other? If one should stray and not stay true to his or her Biblical intent and purpose, will that one suffer – will the others suffer as well?

SEVEN

"Ruth Visits Boaz on the Threshing Floor"

Ruth 3: 1-9

Elimelech_____ ⚰ Naomi _____ ⚰ Mahlon _____ ⚰

Chilion _____ ⚰ Orpah _____ ⚰ Ruth _____ ⚰

Boaz _____ ⚰

The Scripture in chapter six concluded with (2:23):

> *"So she kept fast by the maidens of Boaz to glean*
> *unto the end of barley harvest and of wheat harvest;*
> *and dwelt with her mother in law."*

Ruth obeyed the instructions of both Boaz and Naomi (2:8; 2:22), and stayed in his fields until the harvest was finished. The period of time from the last verse in chapter two until the first verse of chapter three is about seven weeks. Ruth went into the fields at the beginning of barley harvest (1:22) and stayed there until both the barley and wheat harvests were finished (2:23).

The time for gathering in the barley and wheat crops is known as the "Counting of the Omer." It is a period of seven full weeks or

50 days. At the end of this "counting" period, all males had to go back to the Temple for their second required trip to Jerusalem. This second major Jewish holiday is known as Shavuot (SHEH VUH OTE). It is also sometimes called Feast of Weeks because it occurs seven full weeks after the first required trip (Passover). In addition, Shavuot/Feast of Weeks has another name with which most Christians are familiar – Pentecost.

Did Ruth and Boaz see each other again during harvest time? Probably so, but we don't know. Did they ever speak again? Scripture doesn't tell us. But, it really doesn't matter; Boaz made all the necessary arrangements in that first, initial encounter for both Ruth's safety, as well as food for her and Naomi.

Verse 1. *Then Naomi her mother in law said unto her, My daughter, shall I not seek rest for thee, that it may be well with thee?* I believe with all my heart Naomi genuinely loves Ruth, but I also sincerely believe that Naomi would think nothing of using one means to serve two purposes. The harvest is in; all the grain has been cut, so the daily work for Ruth is done. What better time to turn thoughts toward more interesting matters other than gathering in the crops? No doubt these past seven weeks have been very busy for everyone, and thoughts have been centered around getting the grain in on time. Since the harvest is now complete, Naomi has an entirely different agenda to propose to Ruth. Naomi continues to call Ruth her "daughter," and as her "parent," seeks a place where Ruth can find rest – a home.

We talked earlier about how marriages were arranged (see 1:4a). Again, briefly, the father of the groom would go to the father of the prospective bride, and the two would come up with what they felt was not only beneficial for their children, but also mutually favorable for themselves. The father of the groom, typically, would give gifts to both the father of the bride and the bride, and the groom would offer presents of his own to his new bride. With that very basic explanation, let's now look at Naomi's "unconventional" matchmaking.

Verse 2. *And now is not Boaz of our kindred, with whose maidens thou wast? Behold, he winnoweth barley to night in the*

threshingfloor. Probably for the first time, Naomi lets Ruth in on what may have been running through her head since that first day when Ruth "just happened" into Boaz's field (2:3). Naomi said at that time (2:20) that Boaz was "near of kin unto *us*" and "*our* next kinsman." Here in this verse, Naomi continues this line of speaking by referring to Boaz as "*our* kindred." Why is Naomi making such an issue about Boaz being "*our* kinsman?" The answer lies in the little matter of levirate law, wherein a close family member is "obligated" to marry a widow to perpetuate the family name and keep the property within that family. This particular law was one of the 613 commandments given by God to Moses on Mt. Sinai (Deuteronomy 25:5-10).

Let's do a little brainstorming. (Refer to Chart #2, Elimelech/Boaz.) With this chart in hand, mentally "x-out" all those who are no longer in the picture (Elimelech, Mahlon, Chilion and Orpah). (Obed hasn't been born yet.) Now, using logic, who is the obvious person for Boaz to marry to perpetuate this family line and keep the property intact? Where is the initial break? That break, of course, is with Elimelech and Naomi. Let's look at this allegorically and see what Jesus said at this same parallel juncture. In Matthew 10:5b-6, upon sending out his new disciples, Jesus commanded,

> "*Go not into the way of the Gentiles, and into any city of the Samaritans enter ye not: But go rather to the lost sheep of the house of Israel.*"

Then, in Matthew 15:24, a Canaanite woman – a Gentile – came to Jesus seeking healing for her daughter, and he said to her,

> "*...I am not sent but unto the lost sheep of the house of Israel.*"

John wrote of him in John 1:11:

> "*He came unto his own, and his own received him not.*"

Jesus was sent to the House of Israel. There are only a few recorded incidences in Scripture of Jesus with a Gentile. Even after his resurrection, he appeared only to Jews. But, Jesus was not what the Jews wanted. They didn't want a "nobody" born in a manger. They wanted a king and a kingdom, royalty and power. In our story, Naomi (Israel) married Elimelech whose name means, "to me shall kingship come." That was exactly what she wanted. We are not certain as to the true meaning of the name of Boaz, but, just as Jesus wasn't what Israel wanted, I personally believe Boaz, also, was not what Naomi wanted. Boaz was a good man; even Naomi said that about him (2:20), and that's exactly what the Jews say about Jesus today, "He was a good man – nothing more." The obvious proposal for marriage should have been between Boaz and Naomi, "But," you say, "Naomi has already told us she's too old to have children" (1:12). In response to that, I say, "So were Sarah and Elizabeth, and numerous others, but age is no obstacle with God." This is a personal excuse. I believe a marriage between Boaz and Naomi simply is not palatable to her, thus the unconventional, secretive arrangements at night.

All the harvest is in, and the workers have now moved to the threshing floor to separate the grain from the chaff. Threshing floors were hard, smooth, open places prepared on either rock or clay and carefully chosen for favorable exposure to the prevailing winds.[24] In threshing, oxen would drag sleds, weighted down by the driver and possibly others, over the grain to loosen the kernel. Then the winnowers would come in and toss the grain in the air, allowing the cool breezes coming in off the Mediterranean to carry away the chaff.

A few years ago I spent some time studying the most famous Threshing Floor of all times – the Temple Mount in Jerusalem. The background for that particular threshing floor is found in I Chronicles 21:1-30. This Scripture tells us of the time when Satan put into David's heart that he should count the Israelite warriors. He knew this counting was wrong, and was warned by his commander, Joab, that this would bring judgment on Israel. Nevertheless, David proceeded, greatly displeasing God. So, God spoke to David's servant, Gad, and told him to go to David and tell him he was giving David a choice of three punishments: either three years of famine; three months of being pursued by their enemies; or three days of the sword of the Lord in the form of pestilence. David chose the latter saying,

> *"...let me fall now into the hand of the Lord; for very great are his mercies..."* (verse 13b).

During those three days 70,000 men died. Following is a portion of the story (I Chronicles 21:15-18):

> *And God sent an angel unto Jerusalem to destroy it: and as he was destroying, the Lord beheld, and he repented him of the evil, and said to the angel that destroyed, It is enough, stay now thine hand. And the angel of the Lord stood by the threshingfloor of Ornan the Jebusite. And David lifted up his eyes, and saw the angel of the Lord stand between the earth and the heaven, having a drawn sword in his hand stretched out over Jerusalem. Then David and the elders of Israel, who were clothed in sackcloth, fell upon their faces. And David said unto God, Is it not I that commanded the people to be numbered? Even I it is that have sinned and done evil indeed; but as for these sheep, what have they done? Let thine hand, I pray thee, O Lord my God, be on me, and on my father's house; but not on thy people, that they should be plagued. Then the angel of the Lord commanded Gad to say to David, that David should go up, and set up an altar unto the Lord in the threshingfloor of Ornan the Jebusite.*

The story goes on to say that Ornan (sometimes written Araunah) tried to give King David the threshing floor and oxen and grain for the sacrifice, and David said (verse 24),

> *"...I will not take that which is thine for the Lord, nor offer burnt offerings without cost."*

David paid the full price. God accepted David's sacrifice, and David knew that this was to be the place for the House of the Lord God of Israel. That is how the Jews came to own the Temple Mount threshing floor, the place strongly in dispute in Israel today.

Because of the tremendous importance of the Temple Mount threshing floor, I wanted to study all other threshing floors in the Bible to see what other events occurred there and how it might shed light, if any, on our threshing floor in Ruth. This is what I discovered:

(1) In Genesis 50, Joseph mourned and lamented for seven days at a threshing floor over the death of his father, Jacob, and all the Egyptians mourned with him. The Gentile Egyptians shared in Joseph's deep sorrow.

(2) Judges 6 tells the story of Gideon and the wool fleece, which took place on a threshing floor. In this passage we are told of the extreme persecution of Israel by the Midianites. The Angel of the Lord appeared to Gideon and told him that he would be the deliverer of Israel and promised victory through him over the enemy.

(3) II Samuel 6 tells of the time on a threshing floor when Uzzah reached out his hand to steady the Ark of the Covenant, a forbidden act, and God struck him dead. There is never a "good" time to break God's laws. God commanded the Israelites not to touch the Ark (Numbers 4:15,19-20), but Uzzah showed no respect, reverence or godly fear.

(4) Hosea 9 tells about prostitutes working threshing floors. A threshing floor is a place of extreme temptation. There were only men at the threshing floor, and in the guise of night, who would ever know? The wives weren't there; the children weren't there, so why not?

(5) Psalm 132 tells us that the Lord will one day sit enthroned forever and ever on Mt. Zion – *The* Threshing Floor.

Do these other threshing floor scenes give any insight to us about our threshing floor here in the Book of Ruth? Will a death bring great sorrow for both Jew and Gentile? Will a "deliverer" arise who will rescue "Israel" from her enemy? Will the "holiness" of God be approached with respect, reverence, godly fear, or will it be as it was with Uzzah? Will there be the temptation for personal pleasure? Will a "King" come forth? The threshing floor is a very intriguing place. It is to this place that Naomi sends Ruth.

Verse 3. ***Wash thyself therefore, and anoint thee, and put thy raiment upon thee, and get thee down to the floor: but make not thyself known unto the man, until he shall have done eating and drinking.*** So, this is the way Naomi arranges the marriage – no face-to-face meetings with Boaz, no discussions at all of the marriage price? But, Naomi just said in verse one that *she* would seek this "rest" (abode) for Ruth. How is "she" doing that? Why so untraditional a marriage arrangement? Certainly, Naomi desires that her *daughter* have a home. *However, if in securing this home for Ruth she can also meet personal needs, then what harm can there be in her "unconventional matchmaking?"*

Being a clever female with a little savvy as to what entices a man, Naomi tells Ruth to bathe, put on perfume and dress in her finest clothes. We have every reason to believe that Ruth was probably a very lovely young woman. (We know for certain that she was lovely inside.) Boaz probably has never seen Ruth in her finest attire, and he's certainly never seen her arrayed and perfumed entirely for his pleasure. He knew her in everyday work clothes in the field, but what Naomi proposes is a far cry from those "earthy," field clothes with the scent of perspiration.

It is quite possible that Ruth had gone into the fields this particular day and returned home to tell Naomi that the harvest was finished, and the men had moved to the threshing floor. If so, Naomi wastes no time.

Naomi instructs Ruth to go to the threshing floor, hide in the evening shadows and keep watch until the men have finished eating and drinking, making certain that she's not seen.

Please keep in mind that one of the occurrences on threshing floors was the visit by the local prostitute. Ruth must use extreme caution in this "marriage arrangement." Hosea 9:1 says,

> *...for thou hast gone a whoring from thy God, thou hast loved a reward upon every cornfloor* (threshing floor).

Isn't this mission of Naomi's a dangerous one for Ruth? Why would Naomi bypass the conventional method of making a marriage agreement with Boaz? Why are Ruth and Boaz both placed in this difficult position? Could it be possible that Naomi is avoiding her own personal encounter with Boaz?

Verse 4. ***And it shall be when he lieth down, that thou shalt mark the place where he shall lie, and thou shalt go in, and uncover his feet, and lay thee down; and he will tell thee what thou shalt do.*** Naomi coaches her in every detail. This is an exciting time in Bethlehem. The crops are in, and there is so much to celebrate. The work of threshing is hard and dirty, but no doubt the meal was a happy one, and the drink probably quite inviting. The threshing floor was a man's world (except, of course, for the prostitutes). Men could just put aside all their airs and be themselves. Boaz had to be one contented landowner as he settled down for the night. Naomi cautioned Ruth that she was to watch from her hiding place and note carefully where he lay. There was a lot at stake here; Ruth dare not make a mistake. (Remember Uzzah on the threshing floor.) What if in the firelight there was another who looked just like Boaz that night? Or, what if Ruth carefully followed Boaz with her eyes, but glanced away for just a moment, losing sight of the place where he lay? What if she by mistake found herself lying at the feet of another? She would most certainly be taken for a prostitute. And, who would come to her rescue? Who would know the truth? Her mission was precarious indeed.

When it was safe to move, she was to leave her hiding place and go quietly to where Boaz lay and place herself at his feet. Why didn't Naomi tell her to lie *beside* him so he could see her pleasant face and smell the fragrance of her perfume? Why at his feet? What if this "scheme" made him angry, and he reacted by lunging out at her in great displeasure? Lying at the feet meant total surrender and servitude. She was to lie there on that stone or hard clay surface, in her best clothes, at an old man's dusty feet who was sweaty from working all day with the grain. Then, she was to uncover those feet and wait for his instructions. A well-respected Rabbi, Meir Zlotowitz, says that this act was a direct request for marriage, a

marriage viewed as "<u>including Naomi</u>." He says, "Lie down is written as if it were a first person verb – 'I will lie down' as if to say
Naomi's merit will accompany Ruth, and thus identify herself with
the deed."[25] There is no doubt that the method and everything
executed that evening were Naomi's doings, and Boaz, of a
certainty, would have understood as much.

Once in place, Ruth was to await his instructions.

Verse 5. ***And she*** (Ruth) ***said unto her*** (Naomi)***, All that thou
sayest unto me I will do.*** Ruth never questioned Naomi. Is this the
unconditional love she espoused for Naomi in Chapter 1, verses 16
and 17?"

> *Entreat me not to leave thee, or to return from
> following after thee: for whither thou goest, I will
> go; and where thou lodgest, I will lodge: thy people
> shall be my people, and thy God my God: Where
> thou diest, will I die, and there will I be buried: the
> Lord do so to me, and more also, if aught but death
> part thee and me."*

"I will do whatever you say," Ruth responds. Her faith is absolutely astonishing! Have you ever trusted anyone enough that you
would say, "I will do whatever you say"? The irony in all of this is
today's stereotypical mother-in-law. She is always viewed as difficult, impossible, even the enemy, and the world would be better off
without her. I have heard it said that the relationship between a
mother-in-law and daughter-in-law is the most difficult of all family
relationships. How many mother-in-law jokes have you heard?
Were there ever any that were favorable to the mother-in-law? Now,
look at Naomi's parallel role. Not only is she the "mother-in-law,"
but she's "Israel" – the *Jew*! How many jokes have you ever heard
about Jews? And, were any of those jokes favorable? How rare,
indeed, is Ruth. She left her own flesh and blood mother for a
mother-in-law – a *Jewish* one at that – and, now it is to this "Jewish
mother-in-law" that she says, "I will do whatever you say." Is there
any wonder Ruth is so revered?

Verse 6. *And she went down unto the floor, and did according to all that her mother in law bade her.* Wonder what was going through Ruth's mind as she walked to the threshing floor that evening and waited in hiding for her cue? Did thoughts wander back to the time in Moab when Naomi told her and Orpah of the hopelessness of their future? Did she remember happier times when there were men in the house, and Naomi acted more like the wife of royalty instead of the desperate widow? As Ruth walked, was she praying to the God of Abraham, Isaac and Jacob for protection and success? Was she gripped with fear from head to toe? Did she love Naomi so much that she would do anything – anything at all – to give her back a hope and a future?

Contemplating the threshing floor scenes we outlined, do you think it ever occurred to Ruth that the proposed relationship might possibly end in a tragedy that would leave both a Jew and a Gentile in mourning (as was the case with Joseph)? Did she hope that God would meet her on this journey and send the desperately needed deliverer (Gideon)? Did she reverence the man and the place to which she was being sent, and did she have a reverential fear of acting carelessly (Uzzah)? Did she know the danger of a woman visiting a threshing floor (prostitutes)? And, did it ever occur to her that hers might be a royal mission (the Lord reigning on Mt. Zion)?

What about her? Had she given any thoughts whatsoever as to what she wanted or *deserved*? What options did she have? Did she want to glean for the rest of her life as she had been doing for the past seven weeks? She was young now, but what about years from now, could she keep up this pace? And, as to Boaz, the elderly landowner, he's been very kind, but what happens when he's gone? Would the next landowner be as generous? And, Naomi – she wouldn't be around forever, either. When she's gone, how would others treat her then? Without her mother-in-law, there would be no ties to the Jewish people. So much was at stake. Naomi's and Ruth's future hung precariously in the balance that night.

Naomi knows all too well the magnitude of her "matchmaking" scheme. She's calling Boaz to task. His reputation is above reproach, and now it's show time! Is he for real? He is a kinsman-redeemer, and if he truly reveres the Torah and its commands, and his relationship with Elimelech, then he has no other option. He must do the thing requested – and required.

Verse 7. *And when Boaz had eaten and drunk, and his heart was merry, he went to lie down at the end of the heap of corn: and she came softly , and uncovered his feet, and laid her down.* It all played out exactly as Naomi had said. She hadn't missed a thing. Ruth arrived at the threshing floor, and indeed Boaz was there. As she watched from her hiding place, she saw the men eating and drinking just as Naomi had said, and, for sure they were in high spirits. Thank you, Naomi, for your wisdom and for doing your homework. Ruth could not afford a mistake, and, likewise, Naomi could not afford for her to make one. All was dependent entirely upon Naomi's plan and Ruth's complete adherence.

We are told that it was customary for the landowner to sleep near the grain pile to protect it from thieves. Boaz, being no different, settled down near his grain after the evening meal. At the appropriate time Ruth approached, uncovered his feet and lay down. What does it mean to uncover someone's feet? Strong's says this is a disgraceful act and means to reveal or make nude. What would be the purpose of disgracing such a gracious man? I don't believe Ruth merely lifted a blanket and exposed his feet, I think she literally took off one or both sandals, making nude his feet (the proper definition) and, thus, signifying her request. This was an extremely daring plan, but these were Naomi's instructions, and Boaz knew exactly what was meant by this gesture. He also knew the "director." Ruth was asking Boaz to lay bare, or make nude, himself for her (and Naomi), receiving nothing in return, because in a levirate marriage, the offspring goes to another. He would be providing a selfless service for the total benefit of others.

Verse 8. *And it came to pass at midnight, that the man was afraid, and turned himself: and, behold, a woman lay at his feet.* In the middle of the night when the whole world is sleeping, a master performance plays out on a threshing floor stage to an audience of One. The Psalmist says in 121:4,

"Indeed, he who watches over Israel will neither slumber nor sleep."

As this scene played out, great must have been the applause of Heaven.

What aroused Boaz and made him "shudder with fear" (the Hebrew meaning)? Was it suddenly being aware of his vulnerable, bare feet, or possibly the noise of a wild creature that startled the sleeping landowner, or could he possibly have had a troubling dream? We don't know, but whatever it was, it was perfectly timed. He raised himself, and saw lying at his uncovered feet the soft form of a woman beautifully adorned, sweetly perfumed and positioned in an act of complete servitude.

Verse 9. *And he said, Who art thou? And she answered, I am Ruth thine handmaid: spread therefore thy skirt over thine handmaid; for thou art a near kinsman.* I believe this "who art thou" is more than just "tell me your name." This particular question reminds me of the time when God asked Adam in the Garden of Eden after the sin, "Where are you?" (Genesis 3:9). Did God not know where Adam was? Of course He knew, but He wanted a testimony from Adam's own lips as to where he was spiritually – not physically. I believe Boaz not only seeks a name as to who is lying at his feet, but a mission statement. Ruth replies, "I am Ruth thine handmaid (meaning female servant or bondslave): spread therefore thy skirt over thine handmaid; for thou art a near kinsman."

To us today, this conversation is very confusing. What is she really requesting him to do when she asks him to spread his "skirt" over her? The NIV translates this skirt as the "corner of his garment." What does that tell us? Is she cold and wants him to share his blanket with her? She is uncovered for sure, and may be cold, but what she lacks is not warmth for a night, but (male) covering for the family of Elimelech perpetually. She and Naomi are vulnerable – exposed and "naked" – because they don't have the necessary male covering. "They" are asking that he take on himself "their" shame and nakedness and extend to "them" his covering – a swap.

Let's look more closely at this skirt, or corner of the garment, that she wants him to spread over her. The Hebrew word for corner of the garment is "wing." She is asking him to spread the outer extremity, or wing, of his garment over her. What does a Jewish man wear on the wings, or the corners, of his garment? (See the *"Did you Know?"* segment on the Tallit.) Jewish males were required to wear tassels on the four corners of their garment as a reminder of the 613 laws God gave on Mt. Sinai. One of those 613 laws was the commandment to perform the act of kinsman-redeemer when a "brother" or near relative had died. In essence, what Ruth did was to extend a proposal for marriage – one required by Law. When she asked Boaz to place his covering over her, she was asking him to prove that he was a keeper of the Law, as he professed by wearing the tassels. If he said, "yes," then he was worthy of the tassels, but if he said, "no," he was a counterfeit.

There is another amazing allegory in Ezekiel 16 where God enters into a marriage contract with Israel. The whole chapter is a classic, but listen to verse eight (NIV) as God speaks,

> *Later I passed by, and when I looked at you* (Israel) *and saw that you were old enough for love, I spread the corner of my garment over you and covered your nakedness. I gave you my solemn oath and entered into a covenant with you, declares the Sovereign Lord, and you became mine.*

Ruth asked Boaz to cover her "nakedness," to enter into a covenant, a solemn oath with her, the same as God did with Israel.

Naomi's match-making methods may be questionable to us, but there's no doubt she knew exactly what she was doing, and Boaz fully understood, as well. Here, she affords Ruth the highest honor that can ever be paid to anyone. Ruth had no right to this elevated position. She was there only because Naomi "moved over." In a message delivered by Rabbi Gary Shansky, of B'rit Hadasha Messianic Synagogue, Memphis, Tennessee, at Lindenwood Christian Church on January 23, 2003, he said, "The position of Israel at the present time is that she has *moved over.*" That's exactly what we see in this verse. Naomi moves over and gives her own position to Ruth. The sad irony in all this is that everything heard that night and everything done that night – every deed, every word, every gesture, every symbolism – was Naomi's, yet the necessary covering *never touched her.* What great love Ruth demonstrated for her mother-in-law by saying, "I will do whatever you say," and what great honor is paid to Ruth by that mother-in-law.

"When," you may ask, allegorically, "did Naomi (Israel) ever show Ruth (the Church) the way to Boaz (Jesus)?" Oh, dear friend, of a certainty, Israel did show the Church the way to the "Threshing Floor." It is because of Israel's writing and preserving of the Holy Scriptures that we know how to approach our *Boaz* (Jesus). Was preserving the Scriptures such a big deal? See the *"Did you Know?"* segment paired with this chapter. I think you'll find it fascinating!

EIGHT

"The Response of Boaz to Ruth's Proposal"
Ruth 3:10-18

Elimelech_____ ⚲Naomi _____ ⚲Mahlon _____ ⚲

Chilion _____ ⚲Orpah _____ ⚲ Ruth _____ ⚲

Boaz _____ ⚲

Ruth approached Boaz at the threshing floor all in accordance with Naomi's instructions. She "made naked" his feet and then asked him to spread his skirt over her. This was a proposal for leverate marriage in which Boaz and Ruth, in a manner of speaking, would trade places. She asked him to take her reproach and the shame of being "naked" – without the necessary male covering (either husband or son) – in exchange for his own covenant covering. Although this was a "win-win" situation for her, it was a very costly one for him. In our previous discussion of Tamar (Ruth 2:20), you will recall how seriously God takes the role of kinsman-redeemer. God commanded such redemption, and in Judah's family, God took Onan, Judah's son, because he would not honor this role. Later, God saw to it that Judah, himself, honored the command, albeit in a most "unconventional" way. (See Appendix, Chart #4, Judah/Tamar.)

We also discussed in the last chapter the "obvious break" in the

Elimelech/Boaz line. There are two generational gaps on this chart (Chart #2): (1) at the Elimelech level, and (2) at the sons' (Mahlon and Chilion) level. The obvious marriage proposal should have come from Naomi to Boaz, with the two of them raising up seed to Elimelech. Naomi, however, "moved over," or abdicated her role, and sent Ruth in her stead, affording Ruth an unmerited, lofty position. We continue with Boaz and Ruth at the threshing floor.

Verse 10. *And he* (Boaz) *said, Blessed be thou of the Lord, my daughter: for thou hast shewed more kindness in the latter end than at the beginning, inasmuch as thou followedst not young men, whether poor or rich.* Before answering Ruth's request for marriage, Boaz blesses her. Can you imagine the anxiety Ruth must have felt at that moment? She was sent under the cloak of night to a place for men only (except prostitutes), and told to go to Boaz, whom she hardly knew, bare his feet and then lay there, waiting for him to tell her what to do. That voice, that unforgettable voice, once again brings comfort to this frightened, young woman, just as it had that first day several weeks earlier in his field (Ruth 2:8-9). Also, note that he continues using the term "my daughter," even though she has just proposed marriage to him.

He tells her that this latter kindness is greater than the kindness she showed earlier. What earlier kindness was he talking about? It was the kindness for which he blessed her that first day in his field. In 2:11, he told her that he was showing her favor because of her treatment of Naomi and her choosing the people of Israel over her own people. That required faith on Ruth's part, but what she has done this evening required far greater faith. She asked marriage and covenant covering – in Naomi's stead – with no thought of gain for self. She chose him over younger men, whether rich or poor. She, by faith, accepts the role of standing in the gap for the broken line in the Estate of Elimelech. The Scripture commands that he, as a kinsman-redeemer, fulfill this role, but on her there are no commands. Consider this very carefully: **Ruth did for Naomi what Naomi was <u>not willing</u> to do for herself, but Naomi did for Ruth what Ruth <u>could not</u> do for herself.** Do you see grace?

Verse 11. ***And now, my daughter, fear not; I will do to thee all that thou requirest: for all the city of my people doth know that thou art a virtuous woman.*** Again, that strong, affirming voice, in a "fatherly" manner, rather than as a suitor, comforts and assures her that all is well, and tells her not to fear.

The next sentence I find to be of monumental proportions! Boaz says he will do for her *all* that she requires. What is she requiring? For what is she asking? Is she merely wanting a husband? Wouldn't that be a temporary fix, even if he were rich? What happens when he dies? That's why she and Naomi are in this position. They had husbands of wealth and prominence, so if that's all Boaz is promising, then at his death they would be right back in the same predicament. What exactly is she "requiring," and how can he be so certain that he can give her "all" she requires? She's asking for male covering that will rescue from oblivion Elimilech's line. In other words, he has to produce a son through her. That's her requirement. What if she gets pregnant and it's a girl? Besides, she's been married before and didn't have children. How does he know she'll be able to conceive? How can he be so confident that he can fill in the gap in Elimelech's line so that there will never again be a break in this family?

Boaz, with all the certainty of heaven, gives his word that he will do for her all she asks. There is no man on the face of the earth, given the same set of circumstances, who could "promise" what Boaz just promised. But, let's go a step further. Who is really doing the asking? Whose words are in Ruth's mouth, and whose actions were really played out through Ruth at that threshing floor? Were they Ruth's or were they Naomi's? Did he, in essence, have two women (as the Jewish rabbis teach) making proposals of him that night, and did he answer to *both*, "I will do all that you ask?" What manner of man is this Boaz? The requests presented to him are great, yet, he tells her not to be afraid; she has his word.

Then, we have to wonder about the relevance of the next statement, "*all the city of my people doth know that thou art a virtuous woman.*" Why does he care what his fellow townsmen think of Ruth and this marriage? She's going to be *his* wife. What does it matter to him what the people of *Bethlehem, Judah* think? Indeed, it matters a great deal because they share in this, too. You see, Messiah is promised through the line of Judah, of which Boaz and his fellow townsmen are a part. One of these families is the lineage for the promised Messiah, and who knows but that it might be through this particular union? The testimony about Ruth among his fellow Judeans is that she is a virtuous woman, a woman of noble character.

I want to share with you an interesting experience I had that illuminates this statement. Early in my study of Ruth, I had many questions with no answers, and I felt the answers could only come in understanding the original Hebrew text. In my naiveté, I phoned a local orthodox Rabbi and asked for an appointment. To my surprise, he gave me one, and we met at his office at the appointed time. I shared with him that I was doing a Bible study and had several questions. He looked at my list and then reached over to his personal library and brought out a Jewish commentary on Ruth and told me to return it when I was finished. I was shocked that he trusted me enough, a stranger (Gentile stranger at that), to loan me his book. While he and I were sitting there chatting after we'd concluded our discussions of Ruth, he said a most extraordinary thing for which I was not prepared. He said, "I know my son is not the Messiah." I cannot tell you how off guard that caught me, and I was hoping my face didn't register the shock. He went on to say that he was of the Tribe of Benjamin, so he knew his son would not be the Messiah. And, I thought, "Well, of course, if you don't believe Messiah has come, then you are looking for Him in every son born from the Tribe of Judah." Here in our story, every man in Bethlehem-*Judah* possessed the possibility of fathering the Messiah. Who Boaz married was of utmost importance to everyone.

Verse 12. ***And now it is true that I am thy near kinsman: howbeit there is a kinsman nearer than I.*** He says, "Ruth, we have a slight technicality, though, which must first be addressed. You see there is another kinsman-redeemer in line ahead of me." The word "near" in this verse means closer in "place, kindred or time." This other kinsman-redeemer is next in line either because of his position, his relationship or because of a particular time element. We will disclose the allegorical role of this nearer kinsman-redeemer when we get into Chapter Nine; however, just to intrigue you a bit, the counter role of this kinsman-redeemer is not a person. You will recall that in a study of this type, people, things and happenings have hidden or symbolic meaning. The comparative figure does not have to be a person, but can typify an institution, a country, a nationality, a religious system, etc. (as Mahlon and Chilion portrayed the Judges and the Kings).

Verse 13. ***Tarry this night, and it shall be in the morning, that if he will perform unto thee the part of a kinsman, well; let him do the kinsman's part: but if he will not do the part of a kinsman to thee, then will I do the part of a kinsman to thee, as the Lord liveth: lie down until the morning.*** She can rest now; her mission has been successfully completed, and redemption is promised. For the next several hours till daybreak, was it possible for either of them to sleep, or did a myriad of thoughts run through their minds – sometimes clear, sometimes very dark? For her, did she wonder if all of this was a mistake? Was this something *she* wanted or did she feel coerced? Was she lying there thinking about how his life was nearly over, wondering if he could do what he promised, or whether this elaborately staged encounter had all been for naught? Something else – did he even appeal to her? Listen to what Isaiah (53:2b) said about Messiah (who Boaz portrays),

> *"He had no beauty or majesty to attract us to him, nothing in his appearance that we should desire him."*

It is quite possible these same words could have been said about Boaz.

And, what about *his* thoughts? Is he elated at this turn of events, young Ruth rather than aging Naomi? Or, is he sorely grieved in his spirit that Naomi wouldn't come herself? Is he burdened, knowing that this redemption will come by no other means than at great price? Is he contemplating the enormous "expense" he will have to pay for these two, realizing he bears all their shame and reproach and they receive his prized, covenant covering? Is it possible that it's going to take everything in him to pay the price he's promised?

This night reminds me of another night 2,000 years ago when Jesus, in the Garden of Gethsemane (overlooking the Temple Mount – previously a threshing floor), prayed in agony knowing the tremendous price he was about to pay to redeem the world. Jesus willingly traded his garment of righteousness for the disgraceful nakedness of the cross to redeem all those who would come by faith (as Ruth had that night). The Garden of Gethsemane was where the real battle was fought and won. When once you get through the crisis of *will* as Jesus had that night (*"...Nevertheless not my will, but thine, be done"* Luke 22:42), the price externally is of no regard. Jesus yielded His will to God. Boaz vows to Ruth that if the other kinsman-redeemer *will* not, then "as surely as the Lord lives," he *will.*

Another momentous scene in the life of Jesus for us to ponder occurred a few days before his death. In Matthew 23:37, Jesus said concerning the Jews,

> *"O Jerusalem, Jerusalem, thou that killest the prophets, and stonest them which are sent unto thee, how often would I have gathered thy children together, even as a hen gathereth her chickens <u>under her wings, and ye would not!</u>"*

The word "wings" in the above verse translates the same as the Hebrew word for the "skirt" of Boaz that Ruth asked him to spread over her. Jesus longed to gather Israel under His "wings," but she was not willing. And, just as Israel wasn't willing, I believe that night Boaz longed to cover Naomi with the corner of his garment – his "wings" – but, she, too, was not willing.

Verse 14. *And she* (Ruth) *lay at his feet until the morning: and she rose up before one could know another. And he said, Let it not be known that a woman came into the floor.* How wonderful that he's being so careful to protect her reputation, knowing that the only other visitors to the threshing floor, besides the men, were prostitutes. Of course, he doesn't want it said of his future wife that she was on the threshing floor with him. However, could it be that his sensitivity runs much deeper than this? Certainly, he doesn't want anyone to think Ruth is promiscuous, but could the thoughts of his wife being accused of prostitution reopen old, painful wounds?

Let's look at some amazing Scriptures. First, we read in Joshua 2:8-14, NIV:

> *Before the spies lay down for the night, she* (Rahab the harlot) *went up on the roof and said to them, "I know that the Lord has given this land to you and that a great fear of you has fallen on us, so that all who live in this country are melting in fear because of you. We have heard how the Lord dried up the water of the Red Sea for you when you came out of Egypt, and what you did to Sihon and Og, the two kings of the Amorites east of the Jordan, whom you completely destroyed. When we heard of it, our hearts melted and everyone's courage failed because of you, <u>for the Lord your God is God in heaven above and on the earth below</u>. Now then, please swear to me by the Lord that you will show kindness to my family, because I have shown kindness to you. Give me a sure sign that you will spare the lives of my father and mother, my brothers and sisters, and all who belong to them, and that you will save us from death."*
>
> *"Our lives for your lives!" the men assured her. "If you don't tell what we are doing, we will treat you kindly and faithfully when the Lord gives us the land."*

The conclusion to which this "woman of the evening" came concerning Israel's God was quite phenomenal. She said that their God was the God of the heaven above and the earth beneath. He's the God of everything (v. 11). What spiritual wisdom we find in this *foreign prostitute*!

The next passage we need to see is found in Joshua 6:22-23, 25, NIV.

Joshua said to the two men who had spied out the land, "Go into the prostitute's house and bring her out and all who belong to her, in accordance with your oath to her." So the young men who had done the spying went in and brought out Rahab, her father and mother and brothers and all who belonged to her. They brought out her entire family and put them in a place outside the camp of Israel.

But Joshua spared Rahab, the prostitute, with her family and all who belonged to her, because she hid the men Joshua had sent as spies to Jericho – and she lives among the Israelites to this day.

The next Scripture takes us to the eleventh chapter of Hebrews – also known in religious circles as the "Hall of Faith." This entire chapter is devoted to great people of faith who pleased God. Verse 31 of Hebrews 11 states,

By faith the harlot Rahab perished not with them that believed not, when she had received the spies with peace.

In this "faith" chapter, there are only two women listed, Sarah and Rahab. Gentile, prostitute Rahab has her name immortalized with the likes of Abel, Enoch, Noah, Abraham, Isaac, Jacob, Joseph, Moses, Gideon, Samson and David.

Our last reference is found in the book of Matthew in the genealogy of Christ. In 1:5-6 (NIV), we read,

Salmon the father of Boaz, whose mother was Rahab, Boaz the father of Obed, whose mother was Ruth, Obed the father of Jesse, and Jesse the father of King David.

"Boaz whose mother was Rahab" is none other than our Boaz and his "infamous" mother, the harlot of Jericho – the woman of faith!

Was it any wonder that Boaz was being so protective of Ruth at the threshing floor? How much had he been ridiculed as a young boy because of his mother's immoral past? Had he been an outcast himself? Could that have had any bearing as to why Naomi never seemed to want anything to do with him? Was he just too common for her? Had *she* possibly been one of those who ridiculed him?

What about Jesus, Boaz's counter role? Could he, too, have been ridiculed as a young child because of *his* mother? Let me tell you an interesting story that happened to me many years ago. My second job after Ken and I married and moved to Memphis from Mississippi was working for a Jewish cotton broker. On many occasions he would take me out to lunch, and during those times we would have wonderful discussions about his beliefs and mine. I was in my early twenties at the time, totally ignorant of Judaism, and can only imagine what my approach must have been. One day as he was about to leave the office, he took his coat and hat from the coat rack by the front door, and turned to me and said, "Diane, you know there really is no such thing as the virgin birth. Mary was just messin' around in the bull rushes." He donned his hat, took his coat, walked out the door and left me completely numb and with the sickest feeling deep inside. What I really want you to see, though, is not this scene, but the fact that if I heard these words 2,000 years after Mary's conception, then what gossip, taunts and painful words had possibly been hurled at Jesus during his lifetime? Scripture even hints of this during a conversation between the Pharisees and Jesus. In John 8:41, they said to Jesus:

"We are not illegitimate children... (NIV)"

I think they were implicating that he was.

Probably the same ridicule also followed Boaz. For whatever reason, Boaz cautioned Ruth not to let anyone know that she had been to the threshing floor.

Verse 15. ***Also he said, Bring the vail that thou has upon thee, and hold it. And when she held it, he measured six measures of barley, and laid it on her: and she went into the city.*** These shawls, or veils, the women wore were multi-purposed and could be used as a wrapped support for carrying heavy loads, or to protect from the hot sun, or as a covering for the head symbolizing submission. Boaz asked her to hold out her veil, and in it he placed barley. The literal Hebrew reads, "he measured six barleys," not he measured six *measures* of barley, as both the NIV and the King James translate. Six measures of barley would have been virtually impossible for Ruth to manage. The Talmud states that if we translate this literally, it means six grains of barley. But, if we translate it "six measures," then that means "six se'ahs (the measure usually used on the field and in the threshing floor [Rashi]), and a woman cannot carry such a heavy weight!"[26] Grain is very dense; a bushel weighs about 60 pounds – the approximate weight of the six "measures." Ruth could neither have carried this load nor tied such an amount in her veil. We know that she went to the threshing floor dressed in her finest apparel. Her veil is probably designed more for beauty and femininity rather than for hauling.

If the above is impossible, then let's take the literal approach. The Hebrew text reads, "he measured six barleys." The word "measured" is used in the sense of stretching out as a measuring line – a means of evaluating, weighing or judging. We know the importance of numbers in Hebrew. The number six is the number for mankind and falls short of the perfect number seven. If this passage is taken literally, then what we see Boaz doing is measuring something and finding that it falls short of perfection. This unusual gift he presents to Ruth. Why would he do such a thing? Isn't he overjoyed with his soon-to-be wife? He said he was. Why would he give her something that says, "You've been measured and found lacking?" (The answer comes in just two more verses.) She accepts the six barleys and leaves for home.

Verse 16. *And when she came to her mother in law, she* (Naomi) *said, Who art thou, my daughter? And she told her all that the man had done to her.* Ruth's mission was a complete success, and she couldn't wait to share with Naomi every move, every word, every expression, every silent moment – everything. Ruth left the threshing floor before sunrise, and arrived home probably soon thereafter. Was

Ruth about to explode in her youthful enthusiasm, or was she some-what pensive about what had just taken place?

Did Naomi lie awake all night worrying about the outcome, whether Ruth had followed her every instruction, or what Boaz thought of *her* little scheme? Was Naomi relieved that everything had played out exactly as she had designed, or could there have been a slight tinge of jealousy stirring inside her as she listened to Ruth's enthusiastic re-enactment?

"Oh, dear Mother, dear Mother," Ruth might have exclaimed, "you should have been there. It was so incredible – just like you said it would be. Oh, and his voice, it is still ringing in my ears; it's such a melodious voice, like none I've ever heard. My knees were knocking, I was shivering with fright, and when that voice fell on my ears, an amazing peace completely engulfed me. Oh, and dear Mother, the very best part of all was when he spread the corner of his garment over me. It was as if Heaven reached down and kissed me. I can't explain it. It made chills run down my entire body. I've never had anything affect me like that before." Try as you may, dear Ruth, it can never be explained. The truth is you had to have been there – in person. This is the one encounter that can never be expe-rienced vicariously.

Verse 17. *And she* (Ruth) *said, These six measures of barley gave he me; for he said to me, Go not empty unto thy mother in law.* (Again, the word "measures" here is not in the original Hebrew text.) So, the six barleys were not for Ruth at all but for Naomi! They were a "gift" from Boaz designated specifically for her. Could it be that she was the one measured and found lacking?

We discussed previously how in arranging a marriage the father of the groom approached the father of the bride, and if they came to terms as to the suitability of their children for each other, and the sums to be paid, then a marriage was made. We see this order very clearly in Genesis 34, where Shechem, prince of the Hivites, desired to wed Dinah, daughter of Jacob. Verses 4,6,11 and 12, tell us:

> *And Shechem spake unto his father Hamor, saying, get me this damsel to wife. And Hamor the father of*

Shechem went out unto Jacob to commune with him. And Shechem said unto her father and unto her brethren, let me find grace in your eyes, and what ye shall say unto me I will give. Ask me never so much <u>dowry</u> and <u>gift</u>, and I will give according as ye shall say unto me: but give me the damsel to wife.

In that culture, there were three different gifts exchanged between the two families. (1) A gift (dowry) from the father of the groom (and sometimes the groom himself) to the father of the bride. This gift was an obligation of the law. (2) A gift from the bride's father to his daughter. This gift was viewed as a daughter's share of the inheritance in her father's estate. (3) A gift from the groom to the bride. This gift was voluntary and a demonstration of his love. The exchange of gifts signified the marriage terms were acceptable.

With the *gift* of six barleys to Naomi, Boaz accepts Naomi's terms of marriage to Ruth. Naomi, as the "parent" in this arrangement by law is entitled to a gift, thus the "telltale" gift of six barleys.

What about a gift, though, from Naomi to Ruth? We heard her destitute speech back in chapter one telling how she was once full, but now she's empty. It would appear that she has nothing to give as a gift, but that's not so. She has a very precious gift for Ruth. What she gave Ruth was her own position in this plan to redeem the Estate of Elimelech. Oh, the enormous debt Ruth owes to Naomi! The gift Ruth receives affords her status, prominence and prestige. She has Boaz's male covering; she has position. Boaz stands in for Elimelech – the one with the kingly name – and Ruth stands in for Naomi – his queen. Boaz assumes kingly status and Ruth that of his queen.

And, as for the last gift – the gift from the groom to his bride – what did Boaz give Ruth? The answer is found in verse 11. Boaz said to Ruth, *I will do to thee <u>all</u> that thou requirest.* Was that a costly gift – to give her all she required? It was the costliest and most precious of all.

In the following exercise there is something extraordinary I want you to see. Follow these simple instructions. Fill in the blanks below in the following order. First, put the name of the bride on the appropriate line in the column for the Bride's family (Ruth, of course).

Above that, put the name of the "parent," the one who "arranged" this marriage (Naomi). Now, go to the groom's side, and on the bottom line, put the name of the groom (Boaz). Now, above that, put the name of the one arranging the marriage for the groom's side.

The Bride's Family   The Groom's Family

_____   _____

(Parent of the Bride)   (Parent of the Groom)

_____   _____

(Bride)   (Groom)

On the groom's side, the name "Boaz" goes in both blanks. In this marriage arrangement, father and son are one!

There is one other matter before leaving. Note Boaz's instructions to Ruth not to go back to her mother-in-law empty-handed. Every time Ruth left Boaz, she had something for Naomi. If, indeed, Naomi is a picture of Israel and Ruth the Church, then are we to conclude that the Church is not only to be interactive with Jewish people, but we are also to be giving toward them, as well? The answer is just as much "yes" for us today as it was for Ruth then. How can we to whom so much has been given do any less?

Verse 18. ***Then said she*** (Naomi), ***Sit still, my daughter, until thou know how the matter will fall: for the man will not be in rest, until he have finished the thing this day.*** Naomi, ever the teacher! She's still calling the shots. Her instructions to Ruth are to wait and see how it all turns out. But, the encouraging part for Ruth is that Naomi says Boaz will not rest until the matter is finished – this very day. Ruth wasn't the only one playing the waiting game; Naomi was too. The revival of Elimelech's estate meant "everything" to both of them!

Since the time that God spoke to me in 1995 about Ruth, He has opened a huge, Jewish world to this common, Gentile Mississippi-born girl. Before that time I hardly knew any Jews. Let me share just one of the many, amazing stories.

One Saturday Ken and I went to B'rit Hadasha to worship at their Sabbath service. We were handed the usual bulletins as we entered, and sat down and began reading. I noticed an announcement that the Jewish Community Center was offering beginning Hebrew classes open to the public. One of my heart's desires for a long, long time had been to take Hebrew. So, as I read, I prayed, telling the Lord that I *really* wanted to take those classes, but only if it was His will. Then I prayed for God to let Ken be the one to suggest it, if it was His will. I had hardly finished my prayer when Ken reached over and pointed to that announcement in the bulletin and said, "You've always wanted to take Hebrew. Why don't you do this?" Isn't God amazing? I didn't have to be asked twice!

I went to that first class, which was a couple of years or so after having begun my Ruth journey, and was thrilled that I might be doing some of my own research in Hebrew. I walked into the room and was warmly welcomed. The teacher got up and told us her name – Naomi – and said she was a native of Israel. I nearly fell out of my chair. From the very start, she and I became the best of friends, and she has been an invaluable resource in the writing of this book.

Unfortunately, though, my dear Naomi and her husband were transferred to another state. I truly miss our comfortable relationship – and her constant teaching. But, God wasn't finished. The Center found a new teacher, and she came to her first class and announced that she also was native Israeli, and her name was Naomi! I knew this was a further confirmation for this work, and my opportunity (not only to learn Hebrew) to bear my gifts (encouragement, simple notes, baked goods, where allowed, help in moving – anything that translated love). Thank you God! "May we never go empty handed."

NINE

"Boaz Confronts 'Nearer'
Kinsman-Redeemer"
Ruth 4:1-8

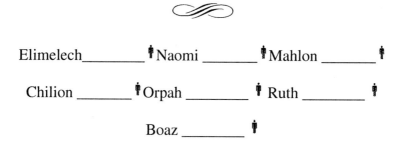

Elimelech_____ Naomi _____ Mahlon _____

Chilion _____ Orpah _____ Ruth _____

Boaz _____

By this time you should be comfortable with the "dual" roles for each of the above figures. Here we begin the final chapter of the Book of Ruth and the unveiling of another key player, the other kinsman-redeemer.

A few commentaries I read on Ruth stated that Boaz and Ruth "sealed" their vows that night on the threshing floor by having intimate relations. To me, such thinking is almost blasphemous. There was yet another kinsman-redeemer in line who *could* redeem and take Ruth as his wife. How absurd to think that Boaz would ever act so presumptuously. And, what an embarrassing predicament that would have created. The character of Boaz is above reproach. He is a worthy redeemer with thoughts only of restoring Elimelech's broken line and rescuing the hopelessness of Naomi and Ruth. This marriage was not one of passion or self-pleasure, but of self-denial and sacrifice.

Verse 1. *Then went Boaz up to the gate, and sat him down there: and, behold, the kinsman of whom Boaz spake came by; unto whom he said, Ho, such a one! Turn aside, sit down here. And he turned aside, and sat down.* We recall from our previous chapter that Ruth left the threshing floor after extending the marriage proposal to Boaz and went back to Naomi to tell her all the events of the evening and to wait for the next move.

Possibly Boaz spoke to his foreman and then left the threshing floor for that "life-altering" encounter. He arrives in town and takes a seated position at the town gate. What does all of this mean?

The city gates ". . . served as the administrative and judicial center where legal matters were discussed and prosecuted."[27] "One of the most important uses of the gates of an ancient city was for the purpose of holding court. Stone seats were provided for the judges. Thus Lot sat in the gate as a judge (Genesis 19:1). The city gates of those days would be like our modern courthouse. . . . The Mosaic law recognized the city gates as the place of justice: 'Judges and officers shalt thou make thee in all thy gates, which the Lord thy God giveth thee, throughout thy tribes, and they shall judge the people with just judgment' (Deuteronomy 16:18). Thus it can be seen that one of the most important places in an ancient city was the gates of that city."[28] The Torah was taught at the city gate; the Sanhedrin convened at the city gate; property disputes, along with a wide variety of crimes, from stealing livestock to murder, were settled there. When Boaz went to the gate, the "courthouse," and sat down, that meant he was seated as a judge.

After Boaz established his position at the gate, the other kinsman-redeemer made his appearance. As stated, this kinsman is *ahead* of Boaz either in position, relationship or time because he is referred to as the "nearer" kinsman-redeemer. As this nearer kinsman approaches, Boaz calls for him to come over and, likewise, take a seat. When this kinsman is seated, he, too, is in the same position as Boaz. They both are seated in the courthouse as judges. We have a most unusual setting. In this courtroom there are two judges presiding, yet, whom are they judging? There is no one else for them to judge – no one to be brought before them – no one except each other. Astonishingly, we have two judges judging, while simultaneously being judged.

Deciphering, allegorically, the identity of this new player was another of those difficult parts of the book. In my mind, I can hardly disassociate Boaz from Jesus, so if there was another who in some particular aspect was "ahead" of Boaz, that meant there was also someone "ahead" of Jesus. To me, that was unthinkable. However, I discovered there was "one" to whom only Jesus could address as "friend" (the NIV rendering), and who, for a "specific period of time," was *ahead* of Jesus. This nearer kinsman-redeemer portrays the Law, and as we proceed with our story, we will see how perfectly the Law lines up with the nearer kinsman-redeemer role.

In the allegorical realm, what we are witnessing in this courtroom are two covenants face-to-face, yet only one can emerge the victor. Let's first look at the "nearer" kinsman-redeemer, representing the Law. Was the Law a good thing? Certainly! Was it necessary? Absolutely! If so, then, why would there be a time of confrontation between the New Covenant (Jesus) and the Old Covenant (the Law)? Before we answer that, let's look at the events surrounding the giving of the Law.

The children of Israel, before their Exodus, had been living in Egypt 430 years. They were very "Egyptianized" Hebrews. How could they not be? Just imagine, for instance, you and your family moving to Egypt today and living there for over 400 years. After that length of time, who or what do you think your great-great-great-great-great-great-great grandchildren would be worshiping? Whatever influence you might have had prior to the move would certainly be greatly diluted by that time, and so it was with the Israelites. Not only did God have to get them out of Egypt – He had to get Egypt out of them! Consequently, God gave His Law to Moses on Mt. Sinai, sometimes referred to as the Mosaic Covenant and sometimes the Ten Commandments. This Law was designed to cleanse and bring back into a covenant relationship His chosen people. They had to be purged from all those pagan practices and restored to the relationship God began with their fathers, Abraham, Isaac and Jacob.

From its very inception, the Law seemed more like a stone wall rather than a passage to freedom. You will recall that while Moses was on Mt. Sinai for 40 days and nights receiving the Law, the children of Israel were down below making a golden calf to worship – *like they had back in Egypt*. They said Moses had been gone so long that they decided to take matters in their own hands and told Aaron to make an idol for them. They said,

> ..."*Come, make us gods who will go before us. As for this fellow Moses who brought us up out of Egypt, we don't know what has happened to him.*" (Exodus 32:1 NIV).

This made God extremely angry. He told Moses what was going on down below in the Hebrew camp, and that He was about to destroy all the Israelites. Moses begged God to relent, and He did. Then, Moses came down from the mountain and saw the people dancing around the calf. *His* anger burned, and *he* threw the tablets down, breaking them into pieces – the very tablets *written with the finger of God* (Exodus 31:18)! Moses demanded of Aaron (his brother) to know why he had acted so foolishly as to make the idol, to which Aaron replied:

> "*Don't get so upset, "You know these people and what a wicked bunch they are. Well, I told them, 'Bring me your gold earrings.' So they brought them to me and I threw them into the fire, and ... well ...this calf came out!*" (Exodus 32:22, 24, The Living Bible).

Moses continued on his rampage, telling all who were for the Lord to come over to his side. The Levites joined him, and he told them to go back and forth throughout the camp killing "brother, friend or neighbor" (Exodus 32:26-27).

> *And the children of Levi did according to the word of Moses: and there fell of the people that day about three thousand men* (Exodus 32:28).

This was the birth of the Law – a birth that resulted in 3,000 deaths. God's Law is holy, without excuse and not up for discussion. God will never compromise his exacting demands. He will not lower His standards because man won't raise his. But, because of His amazing love and grace, He will make a way where there clearly is no way (but God).

Let's now turn to the other representative covenant in the courtroom that day – the New Covenant – and see how God made a way without compromising His standards (the Law). Jeremiah (31:31-33):

> *Behold, the days come, saith the Lord, that I will make a new covenant with the house of Israel, and with the house of Judah: Not according to the covenant that I made with their fathers in the day that I took them by the hand to bring them out of the land of Egypt; which my covenant they brake, although I was an husband unto them, saith the Lord: But this shall be the covenant that I will make with the house of Israel; After those days, saith the Lord, I will put my law in their inward parts, and write it in their hearts; and will be their God, and they shall be my people.*

The New Covenant is far superior to the Old Covenant in that the new, also written with the finger of God, would be placed somewhere out of man's reach. Before ascending into Heaven, Jesus told His disciples to wait in Jerusalem for the "Gift" promised by the Father (Acts 1:4). The Gift of which He spoke was this New Covenant prophesied by Jeremiah. This Gift would be penned on the untouchable heart and mind – and not on breakable tablets of stone. Those followers obediently waited, and on the fiftieth day (note this number), God infused this covenant by His Spirit into each believer. This act enabled weak mankind to permanently house the Law with God's own Spirit as the Overseer. (This was the same principle operating in the Holy of Holies inside the Temple.) God, in His infinite genius, made a way for man to keep the Law – the same unbending, uncompromising Law. After the infusion of the Law internally, man would always be in a right relationship with God. His exacting standards by this New Covenant were satisfied!

Interestingly, at the original giving of the Law (the Old Covenant), 3,000 died by the hand of Moses and the Levites. In stark contrast, note what took place at the giving of the New Covenant (Acts 2:41):

> *Then they that gladly received his word were baptized: and the same day there were added unto them about three thousand souls.*

Astonishingly, when the New Covenant came at Pentecost, 3,000 were saved, the same number as those that died when the Law was given. The Law always brings death, but the New Covenant always brings life.

A while back I was asked to share my thoughts on Ruth at an "all-nighter" hosted by our local Messianic congregation. I hadn't been to an "all-nighter" since I was a kid in school, and it really intrigued me that adults would stay up all night, even if it was a tradition. I wasn't about to miss something Jewish, or something that had to do with Ruth, sleep or no sleep. When I arrived at this Jewish home, there was a welcome sign on the front door that read:

**HAPPY
BIRTHDAY!
TORAH!
&
HOLY
SPIRIT!**

I thought that was a most unusual "coincidence" that the Torah (the first five books of the Old Testament, also the Old Covenant, the Law) and the Holy Spirit (the New Covenant) "just happened" to have the same birthdays. (I couldn't wait to check that one out.)

What I came to understand that "sleepless" night was that on Shavuot (the Hebrew word for Pentecost), it is a Jewish tradition to stay up all night studying Torah *and the Book of Ruth*, because it is the celebrated day when the Law was given. The amazing thing, to me, though, is that no one seems to know why they study Ruth. I went there to share with them, but came away with much more than I left behind. God taught me that night that not only were these two Covenants connected by their beginnings (*life* or *death*, 3,000 each), but they also were birthed on the same day of the Hebrew calendar. Isn't it incredible that some 1,500 years after the giving of the Law – on the same day (according to Jewish tradition) – God gave the New Covenant? We serve an arithmetically accurate God!

The purpose of the Old Covenant was to lead us, by faith, to the New Covenant. Paul tells us in Galatians 3:24:

> *Wherefore the law was our schoolmaster to bring us unto Christ, that we might be justified by faith.*

These two Covenants, now face-to-face in our courtroom, are the same, yet opposite. The Old demands duty; the new, faith. The Old functions externally, while the New operates internally in the heart and mind. "Do I, personally, reverence the Mosaic Law?" "Most certainly!" "Am I able to keep that Law?" "No, I'm just like the Apostle Paul when he said (Romans 7:15b, The Living Bible),

> *...for I really want to do what is right, but I can't. I do what I don't want to – what I hate."*

"Do I depend on my keeping the letter of the Law for my salvation?" "Never!" "Do I, by faith, depend on the finished work of Jesus to keep the Law for me and to keep me in a right relationship with the Father?" "Absolutely!"

Verse 2. *And he* (Boaz) *took ten men of the elders of the city, and said, Sit ye down here. And they sat down.* In order to hold court, there must be a quorum of ten present. The term for this quorum is the Hebrew word *minyon,* and means "the full measure required by law to convene court, hold a synagogue service, have a wedding ceremony, a bar mitzvah, etc." The duty of these elders was to represent all the people at these proceedings. Theirs is the testimony. It is their responsibility to make certain everyone knows what takes place in the court proceeding. It is as if all the people are present through this quorum.

Court is now in session!

Verse 3. *And he* (Boaz) *said unto the kinsman, Naomi, that is come again out of the country of Moab, selleth a parcel of land, which was our brother Elimelech's:* Boaz immediately states the case to the nearer kinsman-redeemer and the elders. This seems to be a rather uncomplicated matter. Naomi, now a widow, must sell her husband's property (their fellow kinsman), and he, being "nearer" (the next in line), has the first option to purchase. There is seemingly nothing out of the ordinary here. Such cases were probably quite routine, this one appearing to be no different.

Verse 4. *And I thought to advertise thee, saying, Buy it before the inhabitants, and before the elders of my people. If thou wilt redeem it, redeem it: but if thou wilt not redeem it, then tell me, that I may know: for there is none to redeem it beside thee; and I am after thee. And he* (the nearer kinsman-redeemer) *said, I will redeem it.* In this verse Boaz continues laying out the case. He says this property is to be purchased using the method of *redemption.* Five times in this verse we find the Hebrew word *go'el*, which means "protector" or "redeemer." The Law obligated this go'el to purchase the deceased's property and marry his widow in order to produce a male offspring who would then carry on that family line. But, consider the conversation in Moab (1:11-13), where Naomi told her two daughters-in-law that she was too old to have a husband or bear children. This may be the same thing this nearer kinsman-redeemer is thinking. He may have thought, "Poor *old* Naomi – she could never bear children again. I'll gladly marry her because in the end, all of Elimelech's estate will be merged into mine. What a sweet deal!"

Boaz tells him to reveal his intentions before the elders and all others present. The nearer kinsman confidently accepts the proposal and announces to Boaz, the elders and the other witnesses, "I will redeem it." (He put his hand to the plow.)

Verse 5. ***Then said Boaz, What day thou buyest the field of the hand of Naomi, thou must buy it also of Ruth the Moabitess, the wife of the dead, to raise up the name of the dead upon his inheritance.*** Suddenly, this very simple, legal matter becomes extremely abhorrent and turns quite nasty. This case is presented in two ways: (1) The obvious scenario was the case first stated above in verse three: Elimelech died, Naomi has to sell and he has to redeem by marrying Naomi. However, Naomi changed the terms for this purchase. The new terms are: (2) This redemption must come through her designee – her Moabite daughter-in-law. "But," you say, "Why is that so bad? What man wouldn't jump at a 20-year old rather than a 55-year old?" "No sagging skin, wrinkles or gray hair, just a beautiful face – where's the problem?"

"Oh, indeed, there most certainly is a problem!" We find it clearly stated in Deuteronomy 23:3,

> *An Ammonite or Moabite shall not enter into the congregation of the Lord; even to their tenth generation shall they not enter into the congregation of the Lord for ever.*

This is a portion of the Law given by God to Moses with which the nearer kinsman-redeemer (representing the Law) is most certainly familiar. Simply stated, if this nearer kinsman fathers a child with Ruth, *the Moabitess* (according to Naomi's design), then this offspring cannot enter the assembly of the Lord to the tenth generation; it even says forever. To him such a union is not even a possibility! He would be producing seed that would be banned from the congregation of the Lord for ten generations!

Yet, this is not the end of the matter. There is another part of the Law with which he is also equally familiar. Deuteronomy 25:5-6 states:

> *If brethren dwell together, and one of them die, and have no child, the wife of the dead shall not marry without unto a stranger: her husband's brother shall go in unto her, and take her to him to wife, and*

*perform the duty of an husband's brother unto her.
And it shall be, that the firstborn which she beareth
shall succeed in the name of his brother which is
dead, that his name be not put out of Israel.*

He is in the midst of a major conflict! The Law – who he represents – says he's guilty if he takes Ruth, *the Moabitess*, but, the Law
also says he's guilty if he doesn't. Do you see the impossibility of
the Law? Neither the godly can keep it, nor the ungodly. Why, even
the Law is divided against itself.

Verse 6. **And the kinsman said, I cannot redeem it for myself,
lest I mar mine own inheritance: redeem thou my right to thyself;
for I cannot redeem it.** He knows his limitations. This is a "no-win"
situation for him. As a matter of fact, it exposes his gaping flaws
that will be advertised throughout the land by the elders and all
others present. These verses clearly show the limitations and
condemnation to all that put their trust in obtaining righteousness
by keeping the Law.

Let's go out of our story for just a minute and illustrate this
point. One night some Jewish friends and I were having dinner
together to celebrate a birthday. We were at a very nice restaurant,
enjoying live music and wonderful fellowship. One of my friends
ordered beef tenderloin for her meal. Our dinners arrived, and she
took a bite and said, "This is a taste I've never had before." She
called the waitress over and said, "What is this?" The waitress
answered, "That's the *pork* tenderloin you ordered." Of course, it
was sent back to the kitchen and the beef brought out, but it was too
late. My friend did nothing wrong. She made no intentional blunders – yet, even in her complete innocence, she broke God's Law.
Do you see the inflexibility of the Law?

Not only can this kinsman not redeem Elimelech's estate – the
way Naomi designed it – but, he testifies that his own estate is in
grave danger. This day in court marks his demise. But, if this kinsman-redeemer cannot redeem, then what redeemer is there who can
overcome such insurmountable odds?

Needless to say, this was a huge obstacle in the study of Ruth, and one night as I was pondering this and fervently pleading with God to give me understanding, I heard very clearly in my Spirit, "Paul," and knew that the Apostle Paul held the answers. So, it is to Paul's writings that we go to unlock the mystery of how one kinsman-redeemer (the Law) could not redeem this "Moabitess," while the other (Jesus) could not only redeem, but could eagerly and lovingly embrace the same "Moabitess." Paul tells us in Galatians 3:5-8 (NIV),

> *Does God give you his Spirit and work miracles among you because you observe the law, or because you believe what you heard?*
> *Consider Abraham: "He believed God, and it was credited to him as righteousness." Understand, then, that those who believe are children of Abraham. The Scripture foresaw that God would justify the Gentiles by faith, and announced the gospel in advance to Abraham: "All nations will be blessed through you."*

When I read this, I was astonished! Abraham had the *gospel* preached to him, which he believed, thus establishing him as a man of faith – a righteous man.

What Paul says in these verses is that God made a way for the heathen (the Moabitess and you and me) to become children of Abraham. Look once more at verse seven. *Know ye therefore that they which are of faith, the same are the children of Abraham.* As we stated earlier, the Old Covenant (the Law) is always external, and the New Covenant (faith) is always internal. The Old Covenant was dropped and broken – external; the New Covenant (the exact, same Covenant) is now securely written on the heart and mind – internal. Ruth was Moabitess from the top of her head to the soles of her feet – external, but, by faith, she was the daughter of Abraham through and through – internal.

We recall the story of Abraham, and how he left Ur of the Chaldees – by faith – looking for the Promised Land. He left his people, his kindred, his customs, his gods, his homeland – everything familiar to him. What about Ruth? She, too, left her people, her kindred, her customs, her gods, her homeland, and everything familiar to her – by faith – *just like her father, Abraham!* God does not look on the outside; He only looks on the heart. I Samuel 16:7 says,

> *...for the Lord seeth not as man seeth; for man looketh on the outward appearance* (external), *but the Lord looketh on the heart* (internal).

All that the nearer kinsman-redeemer saw was an unclean, unregenerate, unacceptable *Moabite* (external). All Boaz saw was a pure, chaste, beautiful daughter of Abraham – (internal).

Verse 7. *Now this was the manner in former time in Israel concerning redeeming and concerning changing, for to confirm all things; a man plucked off his shoe, and gave it to his neighbour: and this was a testimony in Israel.* All evidence has been presented, a conclusion reached, and all that remains is the finalization of the agreement. Sandals were extremely important articles of clothing in that rocky, hilly terrain. It was not a small matter to be without one. Did Boaz take off his sandal and give it to the other kinsman, or vice versa? It's not clear. As a matter of fact, the two leading Jewish commentaries, the Midrash and the Talmud, have differing opinions. The Midrash states, "It is more likely Boaz's shoe, for according to the established *halachah* (accepted Jewish tradition), it is the purchaser who gives the pledge (*Bava Metzia 47a; Midrash*). The *Talmud* records a minority opinion that it was the kinsman who drew off his shoe and gave it to Boaz as if to say, 'As I hand you the shoe, I hand over the rights of redemption.'"[29] If these two respected Jewish sources cannot come to terms as to which one ended up with the sandal, then how are we to *know*?

A dear Jewish friend of mine shared with me that at the conclusion of her divorce in Israel, her husband shoved his shoe over to her. (Isn't it amazing that the traditions of thousands of years ago still operate in Israel today?) That would make it seem that the nearer kinsman relinquished his hold on her, as interpreted by the *Talmud*. However, we recall that on the threshing floor, Ruth uncovered, or made naked, Boaz's feet – her proposal for marriage. By taking off his shoe, she asked him to exchange her humiliating and disgraceful circumstances for his covering. Possibly, Ruth's removing his shoe was a dress rehearsal for the actual event. If that is the case, then on this day, it wasn't taken from him, as Ruth had done the night before, but Boaz willingly gave it. This was certainly the case with Jesus. Listen to what Jesus said about himself performing the act of redemption (John 10:15 and 18):

> *"...I lay down my life for the sheep." "No man taketh it from me, but I lay it down of myself..."*

No one made Boaz redeem; no one made Jesus redeem; both chose to pay the price of redemption.

There's another very interesting Scripture that tells us what happens when an eligible kinsman-redeemer refuses to accept his responsibility to redeem, as did this nearer kinsman. We read in Deuteronomy 25:7-10,

> *And if the man like not to take his brother's wife, then let his brother's wife go up to the gate unto the elders* (she took the matter to court)*, and say, My husband's brother refuseth to raise up unto his brother a name in Israel, he will not perform the duty of my husband's brother. Then the elders of his city shall call him, and speak unto him: and if he stand to it, and say, I like not to take her; then shall his brother's wife come unto him in the presence of the elders, and loose his shoe from off his foot, and spit in his face, and shall answer and say, So shall it be done unto that man that will not build up his brother's house. And his name shall be called in Israel, The house of him that hath his shoe loosed.*

In this particular case, this woman's husband's line had ceased (just as Elimelech's), and the eligible party would not offer redemption. Because of her disgrace, she was allowed to disgrace or humiliate the man before the elders at the gate by loosening his sandal and spitting in his face because he was not willing to share with her what was rightfully due her by law. She then spoke a "curse" on his future line. If, because of him, her husband's line was going to cease, then she would put a curse on him so that his line would cease, too.

Verse 8. ***Therefore the kinsman said unto Boaz, Buy it for thee. So he drew off his shoe.*** The matter of the two judges "judging and being judged" is legally, officially and irrevocably concluded. These are the last recorded words of the nearer kinsman-redeemer. His term of office has expired. Did he fulfill his purpose in life? "Yes." The purpose of the Law was to show the need for a Redeemer and to point the way to that worthy Redeemer. Paul makes that quite clear in Galatians 3:24,

> *Wherefore the law was our schoolmaster to bring us*
> *unto Christ, that we might be justified by faith.*

The fact that the Law could not redeem – according to its own terms – made way for the true Champion. In this seemingly insignificant act of removing a sandal, the term of the external Law has come to an end, giving way to the internal Law. Grace has triumphed for all people!

In verse one of this chapter, we pointed out that Boaz called the nearer kinsman-redeemer his "friend" (as translated in the NIV and the original Hebrew), and indeed, in our allegorical approach, he was. Boaz, as a picture of Jesus, could call the Law His friend, but never could you or I. Jesus fully and completely satisfied all the requirements of the Law. He never broke a single commandment. He was the Perfect Law Keeper. No other living soul, past, present or future, has or will ever be able to refer to the Law as "friend."

What happens now that Boaz has bought this estate? In verse six of this chapter, the nearer kinsman said this purchase might mar his estate. That's true. You cannot take on the weaknesses of others without weakening your own position. Boaz was asked to take on himself the humiliation, disgrace and weakness of both Naomi and Ruth. Let's put this scenario into our parallel realm. When Jesus took on himself all of our humiliation, our disgrace, our weaknesses – all our sins – he most certainly weakened Himself. Do you realize Jesus would never have died and would still be alive today if he hadn't taken *our* sins? Paul said in Romans 6:23,

> *"...the wages of sin is death..."*

Sin brings death, yet Jesus never sinned, so how could he have died? It was our sins that caused his death. Also, note that just as in our story the nearer kinsman-redeemer had a choice as to whether or not to redeem, so did Jesus. He did not *have* to give His life. The sacrificial system in place at that time requiring sacrifices day after day and year after year could have remained intact, but Jesus chose to set aside that faulty system that never *permanently* removed sins. He offered His own personal, righteous covering for our "nakedness" once for all. He *chose* to pay the price; He willingly laid himself down. Nobody forced Him to do it. It is that unfathomable love that escapes our mind's understanding. Jesus said in John 10:17-18,

> *"...I lay down my life, that I might take it again. No man taketh it from me, but I lay it down of myself..."*

God made a way where there seemed to be no way. Jesus paid an incalculable price to redeem, and Boaz, too, will pay supremely to redeem Naomi and Ruth.

TEN

"Boaz Acquires Ruth"
Ruth 4:9-12

Elimelech_____ ✝Naomi _____ ✝Mahlon _____ ✝

Chilion _____ ✝Orpah _____ ✝Ruth _____ ✝

Boaz _____ ✝"Nearer" Kinsman-Redeemer _____ ✝

In the previous chapter, we concluded our court proceeding between Boaz and the nearer kinsman-redeemer. At the matter's end, we discovered the limitations of the first kinsman by his inability to redeem Ruth, even though he held the position of "nearer" kinsman-redeemer. After this startling revelation, we witnessed the agreement reached between Boaz and this kinsman with the validation of the agreement by the passing of the sandal.

We also unveiled the identity of the counter role for that other kinsman-redeemer – the Law. We said the Law, or Old Covenant, is always external – by works – and the New Covenant is always internal – by faith. The matter concluded, Boaz turns and addresses the elders and all others assembled at the city gate.

Verse 9. ***And Boaz said unto the elders, and unto all the people, Ye are witnesses this day, that I have bought all that was***

Elimelech's, and all that was Chilion's and Mahlon's, of the hand of Naomi. In this verse Boaz lists all the property he is buying and says it is "of the hand of Naomi," the rightful, legal case – not the Naomi and Ruth case as stated in verse five. Boaz says he is buying all of Elimelech's estate – nothing is to be excluded. The purchase is all-inclusive. As he wants nothing left to chance, he outlines for the witnesses the terms to which he is committing. The purchase is for all the property of Elimelech, all the property of Chilion and all the property of Mahlon (their land-holdings and all their possessions, of which Naomi, Orpah and Ruth are a part). Although Orpah remained in her country of Moab, it has only been about seven weeks since the three women parted company. We can reasonably assume that Orpah is still a single woman. I believe Boaz would have willingly purchased her, too, if she had availed herself to him. He makes perfectly clear that the purchase is for *all*.

Let's move into our parallel realm for just a minute to see if the same kind of *all-inclusive purchase* ever occurred there. Was there ever a time when Jesus (portrayed by Boaz) paid the price for all? Was there a time when he paid the price for all the "Naomis" of the world (those under the Law), or all the "Orpahs" (those who walk by sight), or all the "Ruths" (those who walk by faith)? These three represent mankind in totality. And, indeed, there was such a time when that all-inclusive purchase was made. John tells us of the purchase in I John 2:2,

> *And he* (Jesus) *is the propitiation* (the satisfying substitute) *for our sins: and not for ours only, but also for the sins of the whole world.*

Jesus, himself, said in John 3:17:

> *For God sent not his Son into the world to condemn the world; but that the <u>world</u> through him might be saved.*

Jesus paid the price to purchase the whole world. He was the atoning sacrifice – the full payment – for *all*. His purchase was, indeed, all-inclusive.

Verse 10. *Moreover Ruth the Moabitess, the wife of Mahlon, have I purchased to be my wife, to raise up the name of the dead upon his inheritance, that the name of the dead be not cut off from among his brethren, and from the gate* (authority) *of his place: ye are witnesses this day.* This verse deals with his purchase of Ruth, the Moabitess, whom he declares to wed in order to produce the needed male heir. Although he's purchasing all "of the hand of Naomi," he clearly states that "through Ruth" he will revive the line of the deceased so that the town records will not reflect a cessation in this family. Then he charges the elders and all others present of their responsibility as witnesses to these proceedings. If they faithfully perform their duty to carry this message to all the people, then *the people* would know the truth, and would be without excuse. If, however, they failed to carry the message, then *they* would be without excuse. (In the allegorical realm, the same is true of us today who have personally *witnessed* redemption. We have been invoked with the same responsibility – sharing with those who haven't heard. If we share, they are without excuse; if we don't, *we* are without excuse.)

The role of a kinsman-redeemer is five-fold: (1) He must be a blood relative of the deceased. (2) He must buy back the property of the relative who has to sell. (3) He must agree to raise up seed to the relative who leaves no children. (4) He must have the resources to perform such a task. (5) He is entrusted with the right to sit as judge in place of the relative. Boaz met all of these requirements.

While half of me wants to shout for joy because Ruth has such a worthy bridegroom, the other half wants to weep bitterly because what Ruth gained Naomi lost. Ruth's position has been elevated far above any she ever deserved. She – the Moabitess – has no right to this status. There was nothing inherent in her to warrant such prominence. This privilege was given to her because her mother-in-law took herself out of the picture, making way for Ruth. In light of this fact, how can we that are of Gentile background act in any other manner toward Israel than in utmost reverence, servitude and humility? We stand in this coveted position not by our merit, but by His grace.

Let's replay this scene with a different ending. Suppose Naomi, as was her right, asked for redemption through the kinsman-redeemer without Ruth in the equation. In that case it would have meant that Naomi would have married the "nearer" kinsman-redeemer (the Law). If, as she boldly proclaimed (1:12-13), she had no more children, then there would have been no room for Ruth, the Gentile, and no need for Boaz. What an incomparable and compassionate God we serve. He made a way where there seemed to be no way!

One of the most amazing words, if not *the* most amazing, in the entire book of Ruth is found in this verse. It is the word "purchased." It is the Hebrew word "qanah," and means "to purchase, or acquire, to *provoke to jealousy*."[30] In other words, not only was Boaz purchasing something, but he was purchasing it for the purpose of provoking to jealousy. Who would Boaz want to provoke to jealousy? Does that unusual phrase, "provoke to jealousy," perchance have a familiar ring?

Paul in his teachings sheds some very interesting light on this phrase. In Romans 11:11 (NIV), he says,

> *Again I ask: "Did they* (Israel) *stumble so as to fall beyond recovery? Not at all! Rather, because of their transgression, salvation has come to the Gentiles to make Israel envious* (to provoke her to jealousy). *"*

In this verse Paul teaches that salvation coming to the Gentiles provokes Israel to jealousy. Naomi chose to "move over" (she stumbled), allowing Ruth to be used to perpetuate this line, which new position, in turn, provokes Naomi to jealousy.

Let's continue with Paul's teachings to see how all of this plays out. Romans 11:12 (NIV):

> *But if their* (Israel) *transgression means riches for the world, and their loss means riches for the Gentiles, how much greater riches will their* (Israel) *fullness bring!*

Paul says that because of Israel's stumbling and falling, riches have come to the Gentiles. Praise God! But, also, Praise God, the story doesn't end there! There is, at some time yet future, a "fulness" prophesied for Israel. Paul says since she has been diminished for the sake of the Gentiles, then how much more will her fullness be when she is fully restored?

It is a perfect and complete circle. In the beginning it was God and Israel. Then Israel "moved over," making room for Gentiles. The Gentiles, in turn, are used to provoke Israel to jealousy, after which she is once again gloriously restored. According to Paul, this "fall" and "diminishing" are *temporary*. In our story do you think *empty* Naomi (1:21) will ever be *full* again (Romans 11:12)? Will she, at some future date, recover from her *stumble*? Will this happen because she will be provoked to jealousy? And, if so, who do you think will *provoke her to jealousy*, and how?

How does one provoke another to jealousy? Is it by, "Goody, goody, goody, I have something you don't have?" I recently witnessed a Gentile provoking many Jews to jealousy, and, it certainly wasn't with that attitude. In the *"Did you Know?"* segment coinciding with the previous chapter, we looked at the Jewish Funeral. I told the story of an African-American man – a Gentile – who attended that particular orthodox funeral. This man was meticulously and fashionably dressed. The day before there had been a heavy downpour, and the ground was completely saturated, very muddy. I told of how this man had stepped forward from the crowd during the burial and had taken a shovel from one of the participants (probably an elder), and started shoveling dirt into the grave. (Actually, it was mud.) That was my first orthodox funeral, and it very well may have been his, too. At any rate, I didn't know that the Jewish men personally covered the casket, and I have to wonder if this gentleman knew any more than I did.

A few days later, I visited this family who was sitting "sheva," (the seven days of mourning where the family sits in their home receiving those wishing to pay their respects). We were in a large circle in the living room, and one of the Jewish ladies, who had been at the funeral said, "Something happened at the funeral that will be fixed in my mind forever." She continued, "It was the most unforgettable thing." Then tears welled up in her eyes and began to run down her cheeks, and she said, "I could not believe that man (our African-American, Gentile man) would help shovel the dirt." Many similar comments followed from all around the room, each echoing the same sentiment, while I sat there with a heart about to explode because I understood what was happening. They were overwhelmed that this Gentile would perform such a lowly, selfless task – for them. That man had provoked every Jew at that funeral to jealousy – by his act of loving servitude. He had dared to cross that invisible, yet ever certain, Jewish/Gentile line and follow his heart. He dared to step out in faith.

After the burial, it just so happened that he and I were leaving the cemetery at the same time. I told him that his actions had truly blessed me. He seemed embarrassed, and I guess he thought I was Jewish because he said, "I'm not Jewish." I said, "I'm not either; I'm Baptist." He said, "I'm Methodist." It was obvious I had made him uncomfortable, and he responded in a tone that was somewhat reprimanding, "I did it because I love them!" Exactly! He brought Paul's words to life – he fulfilled Scripture!

There is one more illustration I want to share on this matter of "provoking to jealousy." Some time back I had the privilege of hearing an exchange between an orthodox Rabbi and an evangelical Christian. The Christian was pounding away at the Rabbi, telling him that it was his responsibility to try and convert him. The Rabbi listened patiently, waiting his turn. Then he responded, "I've read the New Testament. I know what Paul says about Gentiles provoking Jews to jealousy. But, you've been trying it your way for 2,000 years, and it hasn't worked. Now, let me tell you how to provoke me to jealousy. If you'll just love me, you'll provoke me to jealousy."

That was not only an incredible eye-opener for me, but it was a godsend as well. Probably 99% of all of us Christians feel we could never provoke a single Jew to jealousy because of our scholarly, Biblical minds. We're certainly no match for confronting Orthodox Jews with *Jewish* Scriptures. But, every single one of us – every believer – without exception – can love unconditionally. And, maybe we, like that Gentile man at the funeral, will be called on to love them – one shovel full at a time.

Boaz said, "I'm taking Ruth as my wife to provoke to jealousy." Turn in the Appendix to Chart #2, Elimelech/Boaz. This could actually be labeled "Chart of Grace." The fact that Ruth (the Church) is lined up directly under Boaz (Christ) is one of God's all-time greatest demonstrations of grace. Just as Ruth had done nothing to deserve her new position; so, too, the Church has done nothing to deserve the favor she's received. Boaz says he's going to use Ruth to woo Naomi back again, just as God will use the Church.

There's one more point to make before leaving this verse. You may have noticed here the reversal of Chilion's and Mahlon's names. Always before when the two were mentioned, Mahlon's name was first. One explanation given by Jewish scholars is that this order is actually the order of their deaths, Chilion died first and then Mahlon.

Verse 11. *And all the people that were in the gate, and the elders, said, We are witnesses. The Lord make the woman that is come into thine house like Rachel and like Leah, which two did build the house of Israel: and do thou worthily in Ephratah and be famous in Bethlehem:* This verse is the response of the people to the charge by Boaz that they are to be witnesses to the legal proceedings. All the people and the elders affirm their responsibility to testify, and then speak the first of three nuptial blessings. These blessings are not the simple, ordinary, common best wishes one might expect to hear at a wedding announcement, but, rather, they are each profound prophecies.

What does it mean in this verse when it says, "*the Lord make the woman* (Ruth)... *like Rachel and Leah, which two did build the house of Israel?*" Let's review briefly the story of Jacob and his two wives, Rachel and Leah. (Please, refer to Chart #3, Jacob).

Jacob's older brother, Esau, accused him of stealing his birthright, and their mother, Rebecca, afraid that Esau would try and kill Jacob, sent him to her brother Laban's house "until things cooled down a bit." She also hoped that while he was away, he would find himself a wife from *civilized* people, unlike Esau's choice. Jacob instantly fell in love with Laban's second daughter (his first cousin), Rachel, agreeing to work for Uncle Laban for seven years for her hand in marriage. Uncle Laban consented to these terms, and there was a wedding. The morning after, however, Jacob discovered Uncle Laban had tricked him and had given him his oldest daughter, Leah, instead of his love, Rachel. After much heated discussion, Jacob agreed to work another seven years for Rachel, and, thus, ended up with the two sisters as his wives. These two women bore Jacob twelve sons. (God later changed Jacob's name to Israel, hence the "House of Israel.") Rachel and Leah were the matriarchs for the House of Israel, a great house indeed! Therefore, from *two* women – came *two* lines – into *one* great house.

Are the witnesses prophesying that, "as Rachel and Leah brought together two lines into one great house, so, too, Ruth single-handedly would bring together *two* lines into *one* great house?" I think we will see that is exactly what is prophesied.

The second prophetic blessing concerns Boaz. Here it is prophesied that by means of this union Boaz would do "worthily" in Ephrathah and become "famous" in Bethlehem. The word "worthily" translates a force, an army, powerful, strong, wealthy, valiant, worthy. Ephrathah is known as the tribal territory of Judah (the line from which Messiah would come). And, the town of Bethlehem was the prophesied birthplace of Messiah (Micah 5:2). Did this second prophecy come to pass for Boaz? Is there power, strength, worth in your own homeland when your great-grandson is the greatest king ever known? And, what about Boaz having *fame* in Bethlehem? When one, at the midnight hour of his life, rescues and redeems the failed estate of Elimelech – the Messianic line – does that merit fame? By his humble obedience as the worthy kinsman-redeemer, Boaz, indeed, catapulted in standing and fame throughout Bethlehem, Ephrathah. He redeemed the Messianic line. What a force! What an army! What a redeemer!

His fame, however, goes beyond the little village of Bethlehem. In Solomon's Temple, there were two named pillars at either side of the entrance to the Temple. The pillar on the right was named Jachin, and the one on the left Boaz (I Kings 7:21; II Chronicles 3:17). His fame spread to the very House of God and to all that entered.

Verse 12. *And let thy house be like the house of Pharez, whom Tamar bare unto Judah, of the seed which the Lord shall give thee of this young woman.* The witnesses and elders proclaim their third and final prophetic blessing. The first was about Ruth, the second Boaz, and the third concerns the future heir of this union. Boaz announced to the court in verse ten of this chapter that through this marriage he would raise up an heir to bridge the broken gap in Elimelech's line. To this declaration the people prophesy that this offspring will be like the son of Judah and Tamar. How could the seed of Judah and Tamar possibly relate, prophetically, to the seed of Boaz and Ruth? Let's review the story of Tamar and her *father-in-law* Judah. (Please refer to Chart #4, Judah.)

Earlier in our study, we touched briefly on the story of Judah and Tamar; however, due to the prophetic relevance in this verse, we need to look more closely at this event. (The full account is found in Genesis 38.) It seems that shortly after the brothers (those 12 tribes of Israel) sold their younger brother, Joseph, into slavery, Judah left home and went to Canaan seeking his fortune. While there he married a Canaanite (a Gentile) woman, who died after giving Judah three sons. The first son, Er, married Tamar, a Gentile, and because God said he was a wicked man, God took his life. Then, Judah gave Tamar to his second son, Onan, in a levirate marriage (as in our story). This son refused to father a child for his brother's line, so the Lord took his life, also. Judah promised Tamar that when his third son, Shelah, came of age, he would give her to him. She returned to her parents' continuing to wear her widow's clothing, waiting for the promise.

After far too much time had elapsed, Tamar realized that father-in-law, Judah, had no intentions of keeping his word to her about his third son. It just so happened, about that same time, Tamar learned that Judah was in the area shearing sheep, so she decided to personally move the matter forward. She engaged her female wiles and plotted to get the promised child through this family line by whatever means necessary. She took off her widow's clothes, put on prostitute's attire and went down to the roadside where Judah was working. She caught his willing eye, and he *hired* her for sexual relations. She asked what he was going to pay her, and he said he would send her a young goat from his flock. She then shrewdly asked what he would give in pledge until she received the goat, and he handed over his signet seal with its cord and his staff. They then had sexual intercourse, and she returned home. Later, he sent one of his servants to retrieve his things and pay the goat, but was told that no prostitute had been at that location. He was somewhat confused, but brushed the matter aside.

About three months later, word got back to Judah that his daughter-in-law was pregnant. He was outraged! "How dare she do such a thing!" He told the people to bring her out and have her burned to death. So, she sent him a little message, along with *his* personal things, and said, "See if you recognize whose seal and cord and staff these are." To this he replied, "She is more righteous than I because *I would not* give her to my son Shelah." And, the Scripture says, "He did not sleep with her again."

In light of the fact that there is a prophetic blessing in our story concerning the future offspring of Boaz and Ruth, what connections do we see between these two events? The first is that both Tamar and Ruth are Gentiles. Next, we see that Tamar's scheme actually rescued the Messianic line, as did Naomi's. It was through the line of Judah – the same family as Elimelech and Boaz – that Messiah was promised. Because of Judah's wicked sons, there was a fatal gap in the prophesied line. This line had come to a halt. Judah's two oldest sons were dead, and he was not honoring God's design of levirate law by giving Tamar to his third son. Time was running out. In the same way, there is also no heir for Elimelech's line. His two "weak, sickly" sons are dead, and Naomi, personally, refuses to cooperate (as did Judah). Naomi's answer to this dilemma was her own scheme of sending Ruth into the arena of prostitutes (as in the Tamar story) to rescue this line. Scripture also tells us that there was only one sexual encounter between Judah and Tamar. Could it be that the same will be true of Boaz and Ruth? Will they, too, have only one opportunity to rescue the Messianic line? Is time running out in our story, just as it was in Judah's day?

In addition, you will want to note on the Judah Chart, that Tamar, the "Gentile daughter-in-law," bypassed the generation of the wicked sons and was positioned directly under Judah. In like manner, *Gentile, daughter-in-law* Ruth bypasses the "weak/sickly" generation of Mahlon and Chilion and is also directly under Boaz.

There is something else incredibly interesting in this scenario. Look at the Judah Chart one more time. Do you see any evidence of deception being used to produce the heir? (Tamar "played" the part of a prostitute.) Now, look at the Jacob Chart, Chart #3. Is deception a part of this family, as well? (Laban gave Leah to wife instead of honoring his commitment to give Rachel.) Finally, go to the Elimelech/Boaz Chart, #2. Was deception a tool used here, too? Was it deception for Naomi to send Ruth in her own place and put Boaz in this awkward position?

And, there is yet another angle of intrigue for us to ponder concerning the future child of Boaz and Ruth. This child was prophesied to be like the child of Judah and Tamar, which union produced twin boys whose delivery was most unusual. During childbirth one of the boys put forth his hand, and the attendant at delivery tied a scarlet ribbon around the wrist. That baby (Zarah) then pulled back his hand into the womb, and the other child (Pharez) became the firstborn.

In a class I taught on Ruth, there was an obstetrician in attendance. I asked him to explain to the group, "stress-wise," what happens to a baby in the birth canal, specifically his heart, brain, oxygen level, etc. I also asked if in his career as an obstetrician he had ever seen a delivery where the limb of one child presents itself and then retracts and a second bypasses that one in the birth canal. He explained that delivery is the most critical time of pregnancy, with every organ in danger. The baby is fighting against the elements of leaving one realm to enter another, and fighting against time. He also stated that he had never seen the limb of one present itself and another be born ahead of that one. (Since that time, I have asked several other professionals of the likelihood of such a birth, and none has ever seen such a case.)

This most unusual delivery meant there was a battle at birth, a battle for the birthright of the Messianic line. Pharez, which means "breach, breaking out, spread abroad, compel increase," won the battle and the right to carry on the line of Judah, and ultimately Messiah.

But, how does this relate to the future offspring of Boaz and Ruth? Why would such words be prophesied over them? We know

Boaz and Ruth have only one son, so how could there be any similarity to Judah's and Tamar's twins? *Or*, could there be an unforeseen, unexpected *turn of events* when their child is born? Could the prize *marked* for one actually go to another? Is the obvious not always so obvious? Will the son of Boaz and Ruth break forth, spread abroad, compel, increase? We will meet this *son* in our next chapter and discover what amazing events take place at the birth of the son of Boaz and Ruth. Indeed, this is an extraordinary prophecy.

ELEVEN

"Ruth Delivers Son to Naomi"
Ruth 4:13-14

Elimelech_____ ⚲Naomi _____ ⚲Mahlon _____ ⚲

Chilion _____ ⚲Orpah _____ ⚲ Ruth _____ ⚲

Boaz _____ ⚲"Nearer" Kinsman-Redeemer _____ ⚲

In the previous chapter at the conclusion of the court proceeding, we saw the three amazing prophecies spoken over the union between Boaz and Ruth. The first said that Ruth *singly* would build a house like the House of Israel, which was built *jointly* by Rachel and Leah. The second said that Boaz would have standing in Ephratah and fame in Bethlehem. And, the third, that the child of Boaz and Ruth would be like the offspring of Judah and Tamar.

Verse 13. *So Boaz took Ruth, and she was his wife: and when he went in unto her, the Lord gave her conception, and she bare a son.* Here in our opening verse, four very important events take place: a marriage, consummation of the marriage, conception and the birth of a son. Do these events occur over a long period of time, or could they possibly happen in rapid-fire succession? Obviously, the birth of the child takes time, but what about the other three?

How much time might we assume passes from the time of the "purchase" at the City Gate until the two are married and Ruth conceives? Naomi told Ruth when she returned from the threshing floor in chapter three (verse 18) that "...*the man* (Boaz) *will not be in rest, until he have <u>finished</u> the thing <u>this day</u>.*"

Is it possible for Boaz to have left the threshing floor, gone to the "courthouse" (the City gate), held the trial, married Ruth, consummated the marriage and fulfilled his promise to restore Elimelech's line – all in one day? It is not only possible, but I believe that is exactly what happened. Naomi said that what Boaz started that day, he would finish – *that day.*

Not long ago Ken and I had the privilege of attending the wedding of the son of a close Jewish friend. It was an orthodox ceremony, very rich in Hebraic traditions handed down through the centuries. We were given a program to follow when we entered the Synagogue, which was mostly in Hebrew. As much of the ceremony was "foreign" to me, and as I could not read Hebrew at the time, another close Jewish friend sat beside me whispering the explanations for the meanings, symbolisms, traditions, etc. throughout the service. At the conclusion of the vows, and before the reception, we were all ushered into the foyer of the Synagogue where we waited for the doors to open into the banquet hall. This time seemed inordinately long to me. There were a lot of people packed in a small foyer, and I was perplexed at the awkwardness of this lull between the ceremony and the reception. It was a glaring interlude, and I kept thinking, "Could the wedding coordinator have missed something somewhere?" It would have been so simple for them to open the doors to the banquet hall and let us wait inside there. But, no one else seemed to notice or be concerned. Perhaps my face registered my confusion because my Jewish friend who had been instructing me during the ceremony pointed to this "lull" on the program and said, "Do you know what's happening right now?" "No," I said. She told me that there was a private room where the bride and groom were consummating their marriage. That was shocking to me. She went on to say that most of the time nothing's happening, but it is on the program and is a centuries-old tradition.

If we are serious about wanting to understand the events in

Ruth, or any other book in the Bible, then it is of utmost importance that we understand them within their cultural confines. We cannot take Jewish Scripture and shroud it in our modern-day traditions and expect to grasp its depth, beauty and true meaning. Much is diluted; much is lost.

There were no more than seven weeks between the time Ruth went into Boaz's field that first day and the time of their marriage. We know this because she began gleaning at the *beginning* of barley harvest, and proposed to him at the *end* of wheat harvest during threshing time. Both barley and wheat harvests take place during the "Counting of the Omer." (Refer to Chart 5, Passover/First Required Trip to Jerusalem.) Barley harvest begins on First Fruits after Passover, and is followed immediately by wheat harvest, both of which must be completed by Shavuot. (Refer to Chart 6, Shavuot/Second Required Trip to Jerusalem.)

The events in Ruth 2:1 to Ruth 4:12 cover only about seven weeks. However, here in this thirteenth verse, there are approximately 40 weeks – or *ten lunar months*. Even in this pregnancy, we have to get out of our norm. For us, a pregnancy lasts nine months, but not so in Judaism. Jews use a lunar calendar. Each month begins with the appearance of the new moon, or every 28 days.[31] The gestation period of a baby is 280 days, or 40 weeks, or ten lunar months (another "ten" in our story). Our verse simply states they married, had relations, she conceived and bore a son. Are these 40 weeks really as "ho-hum" as this verse seems to imply?

Jewish historians and scholars provide a wealth of interesting information about the marriage of Boaz and Ruth. Not only do these teachings shed light on our literal story, but they are phenomenal when carried over into our allegorical realm. Let's look at some of these teachings. One historian states,

> "Boaz dedicated the last day of his life and the last strength of his aging body to the holy task of preparing the source of *Mashiach* (Messiah) with the righteous and pure 'dove' Ruth . . ."

Another writes,

> "One fateful night, <u>the last one of Boaz's life</u>, the spark of Lot and the brilliance of Judah were united as <u>Ruth and Boaz were married</u>. That night, <u>Obed</u>, the grandfather of David, <u>was conceived</u>."

While another tells us,

> "Righteous Boaz married Ruth and lived with her <u>for only one night</u> – the next day he was dead."

And, yet another,

> "And his sacred seed, nurtured through millennia – just as the seeds of Moab, Judah, Tamar, Boaz, and Ruth were nurtured – waiting for the time when it would explode into the flame of the seven days of creation; waiting for the day when a poor man will come riding on a donkey; possessing all talents and blessing, but ascribing nothing to himself and everything to God; leading all the world under the protective wings of divine Presence when HASHEM (the Name) will be King over the entire universe, on that day when HASHEM will be one and His Name will be one."[32]

(Just a quick side note here – you remember earlier my telling about the visit to the rabbi with my list of questions on Ruth? Well, as he handed me his personal book on Ruth from his library, he opened it up to show me how to use it ((their books read right to left)), and one of the first things it opened to was the word, "HaShem." He looked at me and said, "Do you know this word?" And, I said, "No." He said, "It is Hebrew for *The Name*, and is what many Jews say instead of speaking God's Name." They won't say God, Jehovah, Lord, etc., because they feel unworthy to utter such a Holy Name. Rather, they call Him "HaShem" – The Name.)

Incredibly, Jewish historians tell us that the price Boaz paid to fulfill his promise to Ruth was his very life. According to these scholars, it took every ounce of his strength to give Ruth that for which she had asked on the threshing floor. Her request (by way of Naomi) was for Boaz, as kinsman-redeemer, to save this family line from extinction by providing the necessary heir to restore Elimelech's Estate. Isn't it amazing that Boaz, like Jesus, (according to these Jewish historians) gave his all to redeem?

If the above teachings by the Jewish scholars are correct, then Boaz and Ruth had only *one opportunity* to produce that required, promised offspring (the same as was true for Judah and Tamar, *"And he* ((Judah)) *knew her* ((Tamar)) *again no more,"* Genesis 38:26). These Jewish historians record that something "fatal" happened after the wedding ceremony. If, according to Hebrew tradition, the marriage is consummated immediately following the vows, and if fulfilling the promise cost Boaz his life, then Ruth returned home the day of their wedding alone. She was a widow for the second time.

Let's suppose you and I have been summoned to the wedding of Boaz and Ruth, and we are now at that "awkward lull" in the program, waiting to go into the banquet hall. The conversation is lively and exciting because of the marriage of this prominent man and his beautiful, young bride. As a matter of fact, the excitement resonates throughout Israel because Boaz is of the tribe of Judah, the Messianic line. Suddenly, the air rings with a somber voice echoing down the hall, silencing the crowd, and soberly announcing there will be no banquet today because the groom is dead. Jubilation turns to mournful sobs. Since Jewish funerals must occur within 24 hours of death, rather than a procession into the banquet hall, there follows a mournful, slow march to the burial site.

Let's break from our story a moment and look at a New Testament account of a death and burial. In Acts 5:1-10, we find the story of Ananias and Sapphira. It seems these two conspired to sell a piece of land and then lie "to the Holy Ghost" about the price. Peter first confronted the man about the lie, and the man fell dead. Young men covered his body with a cloth and took him out and buried him. *Three hours later* his wife appears, and Peter poses the same question to her, and she also lies. Peter said, "The young men who just buried your husband are at the door and will now bury you."

The timing is what I want you to see. Ananias was buried without even waiting for his wife to attend the burial. She didn't even know he was dead. The burial occurred immediately upon death. Logistically, it is very possible for Ruth to have married, conceived and buried Boaz in the same day. Naomi's testimony was, "...*the man will not be in rest, until he have <u>finished</u> the thing this day.*"

What role does this baby play, allegorically, in our story? This baby was the promised gift to Ruth from Boaz of which he said to her "...*I will do to thee all that thou requirest* (3:11)." In that culture it was "required" that women have a male covering. It was of utmost importance that Boaz leave Ruth with the necessary "male" covering.

This *baby* not only belonged to Boaz and Ruth, but also to Elimelech ("to me shall kingship come"), because she was impregnated with the restorer of Elimelech's line. She was now connected with this royal family in *triplicate*: Elimelech, Boaz and the child. She held an all-inclusive position!

Moving from our story into the parallel realm, what Complete Gift did Jesus give the Church to permanently sustain her, linking her forever to Himself and to God, providing position, hope, standing and a future? Under what "covering" does the Church (the true believers) find herself today? Allegorically, the baby in the Book of Ruth is the Holy Spirit. Does the baby implanted in Ruth, perchance, mirror the Holy Spirit implanted in believers?

Prior to the marriage, Ruth was suspended in an absolutely hopeless existence. Because she was a widow and from the enemy nation of Moab, she had no *legal ties* to any people or any land. She had turned her back on her family and the land of her birth, so there were no ties there, and here in Israel, a foreign woman with no male covering certainly had no ties. For God to take this "nobody," with all the wrong credentials, and permanently elevate and intertwine her with the "kingly" estate of Elimelech, kinsman-redeemer Boaz, and the offspring of one – and yet both – is too marvelous for words! Yet, is that not exactly the position of the Church today? We, too, before our "wedding" and "impregnation" were suspended in a desperate and helpless state. We, too, were "nobodies" with all the wrong credentials and with not a shred of hope. But, an amazing Man named Jesus looked down on our pitiful condition – our sub-existence – saw our hopelessness, and willingly, compassionately and selflessly gave His all to rescue and reconcile us. The price He paid and the Gift He gave also intertwines (in *triplicate*) the believer with the Royal Family of God the Father, God the Son, and God the Holy Spirit. Our position is eternally secure!

There are some beautiful verses depicting our once desperate, but now secure position as true believers. Paul says, regarding the status of the Church, in Ephesians 2:11-12:

> *Wherefore remember, that ye being in time past* <u>*Gentiles*</u> *in the flesh, who are called Uncircumcision by that which is called the Circumcision in the flesh made by hands; That at that time ye were without Christi,* <u>*being aliens from the commonwealth of Israel, and strangers from the covenants of promise, having no hope, and without God in the world*</u>*.*

Continuing in Ephesians 2:19-22, Paul says,

> *Now therefore ye are no more strangers and foreign-ers, but* <u>*fellowcitizens with the saints, and of the household of God*</u>*; And are built upon the founda-tion of the apostles and prophets,* <u>*Jesus Christ himself being the chief corner stone*</u>*; In whom all the building fitly framed together groweth unto an holy temple in the Lord: In whom ye also are builded together for* <u>*an habitation of God through the Spirit*</u>*.*

According to Paul, we Gentiles, who were once the outsiders, now have the Gift of the Holy Spirit inside us making us fellow citi-zens of the household of God and an habitation for the Spirit of God. We are no longer foreigners and aliens but members of God's family. Not only are we members of His family, but we, the Church, are the Temple inside which His very Spirit dwells!

This teaching is marvelous! In light of the two realms, the literal and the allegorical, both Ruth and the Church, "in times past," were strangers and foreigners, with no hope and no future – absolute outsiders. But, because of grace, Ruth was impregnated with the very essence of Boaz and Elimelech, just as the Church is impregnated with the Spirit of God the Father and Jesus the Son. What Boaz placed in Ruth perfectly parallels the Gift of Jesus to the Church. Do we grasp the security of Ruth's position? Do we grasp the security of our own?

Do we find it amazing that God would entrust us (the Church) with such a valuable Treasure as His Spirit housed inside "His Temple" – us? How did we attain such prominence? Yet, is this really such a new concept? Do you recall the time when the children of Israel were wandering in the wilderness, and God instructed them to build a Tabernacle? Inside the Tabernacle was an inner chamber known as the Holy of Holies, and housed therein was the Ark of the Covenant. The Ark contained, among other things, the Tablets of the Law, which were inscribed by the finger of God. Hovering over the Ark was the glorious Presence of God Almighty. He delighted to dwell in the midst of his people, in that innermost sanctuary of the Tabernacle. It was breathtaking. But, is it not equally as breathtaking that Almighty God has now written the Tablets of the Law on our hearts and minds, and has made this inner part of us His Holy Dwelling Place? We, His Temple, are filled with His glorious Presence. He delights to be in *our* midst, just as He delighted to be in the midst of the children of Israel.

God has always desired to be right in the middle of His people – the Center of attention – His rightful place. Have you ever thought that just as the Hebrew children lived those 40 years in temporary, portable dwellings ... *so did God*? If they were going to have a temporary, movable house, He was, too. If they, because of their sin, had to wander for 40 years, then He would wander right along with them. Friends, have we ever considered that the exact, same thing is true of believers today?

This is our journey – right here, right now. This flesh and blood body is our "temporary housing," and, as God was in the midst of the children of Israel, He is in our midst, too.

But we have this treasure in earthen vessels, that the excellency of the power may be of God, and not of us (I Corinthians 4:7).

However, that Holy of Holies had its flaws. Human hands could reach inside and defile those tablets of the Law. (Consider the time the Ark was captured by the Philistines, I Samuel 4:10-11.) But, not so with the present-day "Holy of Holies." Nothing can touch or defile our internal Holy Place. We are forever secure. The prophet Jeremiah foretold of this long ago (Jeremiah 31:31-33),

Behold, the days come, saith the Lord, that I will make a new covenant...not according to the covenant that I made with their fathers...which my covenant they brake...but...*I will put my law in their inward parts and write it in their hearts...*

God has invested in us a rare and valuable Treasure; we walk around daily with our "Covering" securely in place. This Treasure came at great price, and He's not letting go of His investment. Ruth, also, was given an amazingly personal and valuable gift, the longed-for covering. She need never fear again.

What happened during those ten lunar months from the time of conception until the child was born? There is absolutely nothing in Scripture to tell us. Ruth vowed adamantly in chapter one (verses 16-17) that she would never, ever, under any circumstance whatsoever, leave Naomi. She said she'd go where she went, live where she lived, worship Who she worshipped, and even die where she died and be buried there. Then she tacked on that last little phrase (actually, a vow) that God was to deal with her very severely if she failed to keep her word. Did she stay true to this vow, as she tenaciously promised? Or, did she allow *pride* to creep in and mar that perfect, unsullied beginning? Did a spirit of arrogance set in due to the fact that she was now "queen" and Naomi was out? Did she *resent* her "mother-in-law's" constant "prodding" and non-stop "instructions?" Did she rethink her own position and decide that whatever Naomi got she deserved because she vacated her rightful place? This line of thinking is preposterous, isn't it? The pure Ruth we know would never have abandoned her servant position – or, would she? Sad to say, if Ruth parallels the Church (as she has so perfectly up to this point), then, we know all too well what happened.

Consider the track record of the Church since Israel "moved over" and we were grafted in? How have we treated Israel? Since our "impregnation" with the marvelous gift of the Holy Spirit, what has been our attitude to our "mother-in-law?" Let's look at the warnings given by the Apostle Paul to the early Church, concerning her new position. Sad to say, though, those warnings, for the most part, went unheeded. Paul warned in Romans 11:17-25 (NIV),

"If some of the branches have been broken off, and you, though a wild olive shoot, have been grafted in among the others and now share in the nourishing sap from the olive root, do not boast over those branches. If you do, consider this: You do not support the root, but the root supports you. You will say then, "Branches were broken off so that I could be grafted in." Granted. But they were broken off because of unbelief, and you stand by faith. Do not be arrogant, but be afraid. For if God did not spare the natural branches, he will not spare you either.

Consider therefore the kindness and sternness of God: sternness to those who fell, but kindness to you, provided that you continue in his kindness. Otherwise, you also will be cut off. And if they do not persist in unbelief, they will be grafted in, for God is able to graft them in again. After all, if you were cut out of an olive tree that is wild by nature, and contrary to nature were grafted into a cultivated olive tree, how much more readily will these, the natural branches, be grafted into their own olive tree!

I do not want you to be ignorant of this mystery, brothers, so that you may not be conceited: Israel has experienced a hardening in part until the full number of the Gentiles has come in.

Paul says in verse 18 not to boast, in verse 20 not to be arrogant, and in verse 25 not to be ignorant and conceited. Unfortunately, the Church, by and large, is guilty on all accounts. How, with such an attitude of boastfulness, arrogance, ignorance and conceit, will we ever provoke Israel to jealousy? We've seen what provokes to jealousy, and it is never the attitude of superiority, but only through genuine love, humility and servitude. I wish I could tell you with all confidence that Ruth's attitude in those months leading up to the birth was pure, gentle and above reproach, but on this subject, Scripture is silent.

As stated earlier, this book is viewed from three perspectives: literally, allegorically and through the three required pilgrimages to Jerusalem. When these three are aligned, our story *explodes* with limitless insight and understanding. Let's once again lay our events at this juncture in Ruth alongside the pilgrimage feasts to broaden our perspective.

It was around the time of Passover that Naomi and Ruth returned home to Bethlehem from Moab. Ruth gleaned in Boaz's fields during the fifty days of the "Counting of the Omer," and at the end of the counting period, she visited Boaz on the threshing floor. The next day was probably Shavuot because the harvest was complete, and because all the necessary players "just happened" to be in the City. (You remember that it was Naomi who was orchestrating the affair. She was brilliant, and her timing in all regards flawless. She *knew* Jewish tradition and used it superbly.) If this is, indeed, the case, then Boaz would have held the court session, and gone to the Tabernacle to observe the required wave offering of the two loaves of bread from the newly harvested grain. (You might find it interesting that in Messianic Judaism, it is taught that these two loaves represent Israel [Naomi] and the Church [Ruth]. Astounding!) After this required observance, Boaz likely went for his bride and after the vows, consummated the marriage by giving his best, his all, his promised gift that would sustain her (and Naomi) and forever hold her position secure. All events are perfectly in place.

Let's now break down this second holiday of Shavuot (SHEH VUH OTE) into our four biblical time frames: the time of the Exodus, the time of our story, the time of Christ and present-day

Judaism. You will recall that there were three occasions when Jewish males were commanded to go to the Temple and make sacrifices before the Lord, Passover, Shavuot and Sukkot. (The outline for each can be found in the Appendix, Charts 5, 6 and 7. We reviewed Passover in Chapter Four, Ruth 1:22.)

Shavuot is the Hebrew word meaning "fifty." In Greek it is the word Pentecost. It gets its name because it is observed at the conclusion of the "Counting of the Omer," which is seven full weeks, or fifty days, after Passover. This holiday is also sometimes called Feast of Weeks. We stated that all three holidays are connected with no break.

Shavuot[33] **at the time of the Exodus** was when God gave a valuable gift – the Law. This holiday also requires a wave offering. There was a very unique "wave offering" on that first Shavuot. Moses descended Mt. Sinai and *waved* the *two* tablets of the Law before the Lord. Following was the time when waiting for a specific event to take place, which we call the "marked occurrence," so they could celebrate the third holiday of Sukkot. The "marked occurrence" for the Hebrew children took 40 years. It was when the last person, twenty and above, had died of those who grumbled against the Lord when the Israelites sent spies into the Land of Canaan (Numbers 13 and 14). After that "marked occurrence," they entered the Promised Land and celebrated the final holiday of Sukkot.

Shavuot during the time of our story would have found Boaz going before the Lord at the Tabernacle and waving his required *two* loaves of bread. He purchased Ruth as his wife and honored his word to give her the promised seed to bridge the gap in Elimelech's line. As a valuable gift was given at the time of the Exodus (the Law), so, a valuable gift was given in our story. Jewish scholars teach that this gift, the promised seed, cost Boaz his life. Following this came the time while waiting for the "marked occurrence." Their "marked occurrence" – the birth of the child – took 40 weeks.

At the time of Christ on **Shavuot**, we again see a valuable gift given. Acts 2 tells us that on Shavuot (Pentecost) His followers were all together in Jerusalem, and suddenly there came a sound from Heaven as of a rushing, mighty wind, and they were all filled with the Holy Spirit – God's Law was written on their hearts and minds. The Law (this time internalized) was again the wave offering before the Lord, and the "marked occurrence" for which the believers wait is the Rapture and the ultimate celebration of Sukkot in the Promised Land.

On **Shavuot in present-day Judaism**, many will stay up all night studying Torah and the Book of Ruth. There is no clear consensus as to why Ruth is studied. It is presumed, according to the Rabbis, it is because Ruth denounced her Moabite heritage and embraced Torah. Synagogues hold a special Shavuot service honoring the giving of the Law (the Torah). No wave offering is made because there is no Temple. As for the time between Shavuot and Sukkot when waiting for a "marked occurrence," Jews will tell you exactly for what they wait – the coming of Messiah, the same as for Christians today.

Verse 14. *And the women said unto Naomi, Blessed be the Lord, which hath not left thee this day without a kinsman, that his name may be famous in Israel.* From this point forward, Ruth's name is not mentioned again in an active role. In the following verse (verse 15), she is praised for her love for Naomi and for giving birth to this child, but she no longer appears to be a major player. As a matter of fact, she doesn't even seem to be in the picture. How is it that Naomi is once again forefront? Why is the child called "her" kinsman-redeemer? Where is Ruth? Ruth is definitely not the type to go to such extremes as putting her own life in jeopardy and risking her reputation (at the threshing floor) to get this valuable treasure, and then not staying around for the rewards. Her husband gave his all to give her this child; surely, she's grateful. Why is Ruth so abruptly *out* and Naomi *in*? What unusual "turn of events" took place? Did something out of the ordinary happen at the birth of this child? Did the prize "certain for one" actually go to another? Is this abrupt role reversal the fulfillment of the prophecy that compared this child to the child of Judah and Tamar?

In verse 14, who are these women that are speaking to Naomi? They could be female family members, neighbors, midwives or even the wives of those elders and witnesses who prophesied at the City Gate some ten months earlier. The blessing in this verse (*"that his name may be famous in Israel")* even echoes one of the prophetic utterances at the City Gate that day. Their identity is unknown to us, but whoever they are, they praise the Lord for His unfailing love *to Naomi*, because on "this day" Naomi has *her* kinsman-redeemer.

What is "this day?" And, why is "this" such an important day? This is probably the birthday of the child. *It is my position* that just as the giving of this child cost Boaz his life, so, the birthing of this child cost Ruth hers. This would definitely present an unusual *turn of events* at the birth. Ruth was, for certain, the one *marked* for the prize, just as the twin son of Judah and Tamar with the scarlet ribbon around his wrist was the one *marked* for the prize. "But," you say, "that's cruel to say that Ruth died; we don't know that." Viewing this book with only the information found in the four chapters of Ruth leaves many unanswered questions. However, when we broaden the perspective and go outside the box into the other realms, Ruth's "death" is not cruel at all. On the contrary, it is victorious and *necessary*!

Listen to the words Jesus spoke concerning the first giving of *this child* (the Holy Spirit) in John 16:7,

> *"Nevertheless I tell you the truth; <u>It is expedient for you that I go away; for if I go not away, the Comforter will not come unto you; but if I depart, I will send him unto you.</u>"*

For whatever reason, the Gift of the Holy Spirit could not be given to the Church as long as Jesus was physically present. He had to step aside and make way. Would we give complete allegiance and total surrender to the Holy Spirit if Jesus were still present? Had he remained behind, would we ever have learned to use our spiritual eyes, or, rather, would we have always been looking with our physical eyes for the visible Jesus? And, if Ruth were still on the scene, the child would have clung to his mother, but that was not God's plan. Ruth's exit was absolutely necessary, for now it is all about Naomi.

In the allegorical realm, what is the "marked occurrence" for the Church? What is that greatly anticipated time for which she waits? You will notice on Chart 6, the Second Required Trip to Jerusalem, that following Shavuot there is a time of waiting for a "marked occurrence." Only on Jewish calendars is this a set time. At the time of the Exodus, the "marked occurrence" took 40 years. At the time in our story, the "marked occurrence" took 40 weeks. For us today, the "marked occurrence" will be when the Church reaches "full term" and is raptured. "Full term" for the Hebrew children wandering in the wilderness meant the time when the last had died of those twenty years old and above. "Full Term" in Ruth was the time when the baby reached maturity in the womb. And, as for the Christian today, full term is:

> *For I would not, brethren, that ye should be ignorant of this mystery, lest ye should be wise in your own conceits; that blindness in part is happened to Israel, until the **fulness of the Gentiles be come in*** (Romans 11:25).

The Church, too, must reach her maturity – her "full term" – before the long-awaited "marked occurrence."

Is it truly such a sad thing for the Church to reach "full term" and be raptured? Not to those of us who proudly carry about in our earthly Temples the Law and the Spirit of the Lord. As a matter of fact, "We can hardly wait!"

There's a wonderful story I want to share here that is just too good to miss. Do you recall earlier on in this book when I told of the time Ken and I went to that first Passover Seder hosted by the Messianic Congregation? Before that event, I had to go over and pick up the tickets, and you may remember that I was extremely apprehensive about their beliefs and whether or not they were biblically sound. When I arrived at the Synagogue, Anne, the Jewish secretary, greeted me cheerfully. She was very accommodating and seemed excited that we were going to join them for the Seder. She and I were in a small room with a window, and I decided to "test the spirits to see if they were of God" (I John 4:1). So, I said to Anne, "Do you think the Lord's return will be soon?" Without even the slightest hint of hesitation, she turned to the window behind her and pulled aside the curtain. She peered up into the sky, and with such longing as I've never seen before or since said, "I look for Him every morning." (She definitely silenced this skeptic.) What a "marked occurrence" that will be, and how we long for that event!

The absence of Ruth is anything but sad. It is glorious in every respect. It is the absolute best for her, and it is the absolute best for Naomi. God always has our very best at heart. Let's look a second time at Romans 11:25-26a to see what happens in our parallel realm after Ruth's (the Church's) exit.

> *"For I would not, brethren, that ye should be igno-rant of this mystery, lest ye should be wise in your own conceits; that blindness in part is happened to Israel, until the fulness of the Gentiles be come in.* ***And so <u>all</u> Israel shall be saved...*"*

The Rapture of the Church (Ruth's exit) ushers in the restoration of Israel (Naomi) – in totality!

Let your imaginations wander for just a minute back to the time when Boaz and Ruth pledged their vows to each other. How sad, indeed, to think of their never making it into the "banquet hall" or having a "honeymoon." That means Ruth (paralleling the Church) is long overdue for her wedding celebration and for personal, inti-mate times with her beloved. Can the Church expect such a celebra-tion after her "marked occurrence?" John, in the Book of Revelation, pens a beautiful scene yet future (Revelation 19:7-9).

> *Let us be glad and rejoice, and give honour to him: for the marriage of the Lamb is come, and his wife hath made herself ready. And to her was granted that she should be arrayed in fine linen, clean and white: for they which are called unto the marriage supper of the Lamb. And he said unto me, these are the true sayings of God.*

Rather than our being saddened about Ruth's departure, we should rejoice for both Ruth and Naomi. While Ruth is celebrating,

Naomi at long last is embracing *her* kinsman-redeemer.

Here in Ruth 4:14, it is prophesied that this child's name will be famous in Israel. In our story, is this child, indeed, destined for fame? Most certainly! How could the grandfather of the greatest earthly king the world has ever known not find fame in that role? One of the honors bestowed upon a grandfather is to hold his grandson during the covenant of circumcision (the *"Did you Know?"* segment corresponding with this chapter). How special it must have been to be the grandfather of the one of whom it was said, *"He was a man after God's own heart"* (I Samuel 13:14). That would make any grandfather extremely proud. This child Naomi holds will become the "famous" grandfather of King David, the lineage of Messiah.

Yet, while this is a marvelous prophecy in the literal realm, it is a prophecy of unparalleled proportions in the allegorical realm. In that sphere it is said that the Holy Spirit (the child) will become famous in Israel, and what fame that will be when "<u>all</u> Israel is saved (Romans 11:26a)!"

In bringing this chapter to a close, and in light of what we've learned, let's look one final time at those three prophecies spoken that day at the City gate and view their allegorical fulfillment. In Ruth 4:11-12, it was prophesied (1) that Ruth would be like the two, Rachel and Leah, who built the House of Israel; (2) that Boaz would have standing in Ephratah and be famous in Bethlehem; and (3) that the child would be like Pharez, son of Judah and Tamar.

(1) How did Ruth fulfill this prophecy of building a great house comparable to the House of Israel, and are there two "segments" to *this* "house?" This child she carried in her womb was her surety and covering given by Boaz. Boaz promised he would give her all for which she asked. Then, at the City gate, he announced to the elders and witnesses that he was "purchasing" Ruth for the purpose of redeeming the line of Elimelech (4:10). He gave Ruth his word on the threshing floor, and he proclaimed his intentions that day in court. Were there scoffers who chided Ruth during her pregnancy? Did they taunt her with, "You know that's probably a no-account girl in your belly – ha, ha, ha." Did they laugh at her for marrying and burying her "old man" in the same day? How often did Satan try to bring her down with his heinous lies and painful accusations?

The answer can be found in your life and mine. How often does our adversary, the devil, try and tell us that our faith is in vain? Have all of us been tempted to give up because, "It's just too hard, and we're not sure it's worth it?" The fruit in Ruth's womb was the perfect covering for her journey, and at journey's end, this same fruit would also be the perfect covering for Naomi. The fruit in this one womb brings two women (Naomi and Ruth) into one great house, the House of Elimelech (Almighty God).

Does Scripture teach that the Church will bring together two into one? We find written in Paul's letter to the Ephesians (2:13-15 NIV):

> *"But now in Christ Jesus you* (Gentiles) *who once were far away have been brought near through the blood of Christ.*
>
> *For he himself is our peace, who has made the two one* (Jew and Gentile) *and has destroyed the barrier, the dividing wall of hostility, by abolishing in his flesh the law with its commandments and regulations. His purpose was to create in himself one new man out of the two, thus making peace..."*

Paul writes that because of the division (partition) between Jew and Gentile, Jesus paid the price, through His sacrificial death, to bring the two into one, making one new man of the household of faith. As Rachel and Leah were the "vessels" used by the *fruit of their womb* to produce the House of Israel (two for one), so Ruth (portraying the Church) is the "vessel" impregnated with the child (the Holy Spirit) to provoke to jealousy until such time when the partition comes down and Naomi (all Israel) will be saved (one for two). Have the two been brought into one, as foretold by Paul, and do we see that one new man today? Not yet, my friend, but God's Word is certain, and this surely will come to pass.

(2) The second prophecy concerned Boaz (Jesus) achieving standing in Ephratah and fame in Bethlehem. How does Boaz, though dead, become famous? Although this has primarily been covered, there is another important passage at which we need to

look that sheds some additional light. The Prophet Micah speaks a profound word in 5:2,

> *"But thou, Bethlehem Ephratah, though thou be little among the thousands of Judah, yet out of thee shall he come forth unto me that is to be ruler in Israel; whose goings forth have been <u>from of old, from everlasting</u>."*

These words were written some seven centuries before Christ. It says that out of Bethlehem will come one "who is from of old, from everlasting." How can one come out of the little town of Bethlehem whose origins are from eternity past? The answer is, "by way of a manger." Who can understand the mind of God? His design from the foundation of the earth was to clothe Himself as a mortal, be born in Bethlehem and ascend Israel's throne. This verse can refer to none other than Jesus.

Has the prophecy been fulfilled that Jesus (portrayed by Boaz) is famous and has standing (a force, an army, powerful, strong, wealthy, valiant, worthy) in Israel? Sad to say, the answer is, "No." Many Jews refuse to even speak His Name. They deny his "messianic" birth. But, the time will come when this will be fulfilled. However, for our story, it is the next two verses in this passage from the Prophet Micah that are the most intriguing (5:3-4).

> *"<u>Therefore</u> will he give them up, until the time that she which travaileth hath brought forth: <u>then</u> the remnant of his brethren shall return unto the children of Israel. And he shall stand and feed in the strength of the Lord, in the majesty of the name of the Lord his God; and they shall abide: for <u>now</u> shall he be great unto the ends of the earth."*

Micah says, *"therefore,"* meaning that what is about to be said is based on what was just spoken in the previous verse (2). *Therefore*, (because of the Messiah from everlasting coming out of Bethlehem), the Children of Israel will be "given up" until *another*

153

birth takes place. At that time – at that "next birth" – the remnant of the Jews will return to Israel, and *The Lord* will stand and feed, and *His* Name will be great to the ends of the earth.

What is this second birth to which Micah refers that changes the whole landscape of Israel? Could it possibly be the time when the Church travails in birth pains and delivers? At that time will Christian believers deliver the same "Baby" (the Holy Spirit) over to Israel that was delivered to her when Jesus said He had to go away so He could send the "Comforter" (our Surety, our Covering)? This prophecy is yet to be fulfilled, but I believe many alive today could easily see its fulfillment.

Paul in the New Testament also speaks of that "other" birth. In Romans 8:22-23, he says:

> *We know that the whole creation has been groaning as in the pains of childbirth right up to the present time. Not only so, but we ourselves, who have the firstfruits of the Spirit, groan inwardly as we wait eagerly for our adoption as sons, the redemption of our bodies* (NIV).

Ruth waited eagerly for the birth of this child, the birth that would validate her faith.

(3) We've also looked at the extraordinary circumstances surrounding the birth of Pharez – that unusual *turn of events* and the *prize marked for one going to another*, but what we haven't looked at is his life beyond that notable birth. We are told that Pharez became the head of the leading clan in Judah. For these elders and witnesses to prophesy that this offspring (the son of Boaz and Ruth), would become the head of the Tribe of Judah, as was Pharez, was a profound prophecy. They could not have imagined that not only through this offspring would worthy leadership come for their tribe, but it would also extend to the whole House of Israel. The one over whom they prophesied would restore the broken "kingly" line of Elimelech and would become the grandfather of King David.

How many times did David run home after conquests to tell his Granddaddy all the news? Was that possibly one of his first stops after killing giant Goliath? Did David go to Granddaddy for counsel all those many times he was running from King Saul? Was it in those elderly arms that young David found solace and strength? Did David run there to share with him about being made King of Judah, then King of Israel, and finally King over all the land God had originally promised their forefathers? Did he go there to confess his adultery and his having Bathsheba's husband, Uriah, put on the front lines for certain death? Was it on those knees that he wept when in judgment the hand of God came crashing down with the death of his son, Absalom?

Three amazing prophecies – three incredible fulfillments – literally and allegorically! How could those elders and witnesses at the City gate that day ever have imagined the far-reaching scope of their prophetic blessings? They couldn't. They spoke God's word faithfully, and God fulfilled their prophecies divinely.

TWELVE

"Son Restores Naomi"
Ruth 4:15-22

Elimelech_____ ⚣Naomi _____ ⚣Mahlon _____ ⚣

Chilion _____ ⚣Orpah _____ ⚣Ruth _____ ⚣

Boaz _____ ⚣"Nearer" Kinsman-Redeemer _____ ⚣

Obed _____ ⚣

As we bring our study to a close, you will notice the final member is added to the cast. Obed, allegorically the Holy Spirit, takes his place alongside the other notables. For the believer, the Holy Spirit is not only our ever-faithful, constant Companion and Chaperone as we go through this journey, but He is our Sure Deliverer who escorts us safely into the Heavenly Kingdom. It is of the incomparable Spirit of God that Jesus said in Mark 3:28-29 (NIV):

> *"I tell you the truth, all the sins and blasphemies of men will be forgiven them. But whosoever blasphemes against the Holy Spirit will never be forgiven; he is guilty of an eternal sin."*

Our final cast member is undeniably important and is to be given reverential deference.

What a distinguished assemblage, not only literally, but allegorically. In the latter realm we have God, Israel, the Judges, the Kings, non-believers, the true Church, Jesus, the Law and the Holy Spirit. All essentials of both Judaism and Christianity – past, present and future – are accounted for.

We said that the Book of Ruth is a vast storehouse when viewed literally, allegorically and when paralleled with the three major feasts. Literally, our story lasts about 40 weeks after Boaz performed the task of kinsman-redeemer. At the time of the Exodus, the Hebrews' journey spanned some 40 years. And, as for us today, the journey of the true Church has covered some 2,000 years.

Each journey is unique to its own traveler. God was faithful to the Hebrew children, corporately and individually. He never allowed so much as even a pair of sandals or a suit of clothing to wear out in all those forty years. Likewise, God was faithful to Naomi and Ruth, giving position and security to both through the promised child. Even so, He is equally faithful to us. All journeys come with major trials and testings, with resulting consequences or rewards. As the journey for the Israelite children had an end, so did Naomi's and Ruth's, and so will yours and mine. Just as a celebration awaited the Hebrew children in the Promised Land (Sukkot), so a celebration awaits the faithful today. However, not all who make the journey will be allowed into that celebration. Listen to what Jesus said in Matthew 7:21:

> *Not every one that saith unto me, Lord, Lord, shall*
> *enter into the kingdom of heaven.*

On that day, each of us, individually, will stand before the Lord. All of us will greet Him with, "Lord, Lord," but it will not be what comes from our mouths that proves relationship. It will be what's written on our hearts and minds – the core of our being. (God doesn't look on the outward appearance; He looks on the heart, I Samuel 16:7.) If He doesn't see the blood-bought Covenant etched on our hearts and minds, then will be heard,

"I never knew you: depart from me" (Matthew 7:23).

Let's now turn to the last few verses of chapter four to see if Naomi makes it to the "Promised Land." You will recall from the previous chapter that the promised male child has been safely delivered, and Ruth is no longer present. All that remains are Naomi (Israel) and the child (the Holy Spirit).

Verse 15. ***And he*** (the child) ***shall be unto thee*** (Naomi) ***a restorer of thy life, and a nourisher of thine old age: for thy daughter in law, which loveth thee, which is better to thee than seven sons, hath born him.*** The women continue prophesying. To Naomi they say, "This child will restore your life." The Hebrew word for "restore" is similar to that of turning back time, not necessarily to the starting point, but possibly to a time when one veers off course. How many of us would love to have the clock turned back to a particular point in our lives so we could have a second chance, a new beginning? That's exactly what is prophesied for Naomi; that's what this child will do for her.

They further prophesy that the child will "nourish her in her old age." Even though in some aspect she's had the clock turned back, she is still in the final stages of her life. Why does she need to be nourished? The Hebrew word here means to "hold in," to "contain, feed, make provision, provide sustenance." Isn't it amazing that it would be said of an infant – a brand new baby, "This 'child' will *hold, contain, feed, provide,* and *sustain* her (the elder)?" What a mystifying prophecy! Why would Naomi (Israel) need protection and provision? The reason, allegorically, is there are only seven years remaining for those on the earth. Listen to what Jesus says about that time in Matthew 24:21,

> *"For then there will be great tribulation, unequaled from the beginning of the world until now – and never to be equaled again.*

Will this "gift" from Boaz (Jesus), this child (the Holy Spirit), be able to sustain and nourish Naomi (Israel), to hold her in, contain her and feed her through such an horrendous time as foretold by Jesus? Without a doubt!

There is actually a very unique phenomenon playing out at this juncture in our story that I really want you to see. In Jewish tradition when a death occurs, there is an observed time of mourning for seven days. It is called "sheva" because the Hebrew word for seven is sheva. Naomi, however, has not one, but two "sevens" running simultaneously at this point in her life. She has the seven days of sitting sheva, mourning for Ruth, and also the seven days of waiting for the child's circumcision and naming. Let's look at these two "sevens."

The seven days of siting sheva are a very confining, mournful time in Jewish life. This seven-day Jewish tradition begins immediately after the burial. Note from Scripture Joseph's time of sitting sheva for his father Jacob in Genesis 50:10:

> *And they came to the threshingfloor of Atad, which is beyond Jordan, and there they mourned with a great and very sore lamentation: and he made a mourning for his father <u>seven days</u>.*

When sitting sheva, the family will customarily take off their shoes, tear their shirts or blouses (usually a collar or pocket), and sit low on the floor (a sign of humility) in the home of the deceased (if possible). It is not a time for thinking of self. There is no fixing of the hair, no shaving, no makeup. The family sits in this humbled position from early morning until sundown. Mourners do not actually have to sit still for seven days; they are free to move about the house, but the image is one of motionlessness while grieving, remembering, weeping, dreaming, telling stories and sharing memories. Mourners do not work or play. They do not call the office, wash dishes or watch TV. They do not cook, run errands or attend school. Mourners abstain from pleasures of all kinds: sensual, sexual and intellectual. Mourners are not even supposed to read the Torah, because that is considered one of life's greatest joys. Sitting sheva is for the purpose of making a "kind of restitution," and for exploring the whole emotional gamut of <u>regret</u>, relief, <u>guilt</u>, anger, <u>shame</u>, self-pity and <u>remorse</u>.[34] So, we see when sitting sheva that life is on hold and a healing is taking place.

With that said, let's now turn to the second "seven" also running simultaneously in Naomi's life – the time from the birth of the child until he is circumcised and named on the eighth day – when all becomes official. For, indeed, Naomi does have within her grasp the "restorer of her life," and the "nourisher of her old age," but all is not final until she reaches that eighth day.

How can Naomi grieve the death of Ruth while being jubilant over the birth of *her* son? How does she deal with the extremes of mourning on the one hand and rejoicing on the other? Who's sitting sheva? Who's cuddling the baby? Who's receiving mourners? Who's showing off the new kinsman-redeemer? At what moment is she sobbing with regret, guilt, shame and remorse, and at what moment is she peering into the eyes of the one who in reality holds her? It is a bittersweet time in our story, an excruciatingly difficult time, yet an exhilaratingly joyous one.

Let's go forward at this same point into our parallel realm. Ruth, (the Church) is gone during the seven years of the great tribulation when Naomi (Israel) is forced to remember, to grieve, to make restitution. Who will "sit sheva" with Israel? Who will bring her food? (She's not allowed to do it herself.) Who will visit her and comfort her while she grieves over the years of "famine," the years of "death," the years of "alienation," the years of "marah" (bitterness), the years of deceit? Who will rejoice with her as she proclaims the faithfulness of the Redeemer? Who will share with her in her enthusiasm? The answer is the all-sufficient Holy Spirit. The Spirit of Almighty God will nourish her, comfort her, rejoice with her, hold her and hear her confessions. She will hold in her bosom her sure Defense, her strong and mighty Tower, her safe Deliverer. She will not grieve or rejoice alone.

How difficult will those days be? Is it possibly also a difficult time here in our story in Ruth? Could it be that someone is trying to tear the child from Naomi because she doesn't *deserve* this child or doesn't "yet" *own* this child? Remember, all is not official until day eight. This child inherits both the combined estates of Elimelech and Boaz. The three, Elimelech, Boaz and Obed, are as one, an incredible Tower of strength. Is this child of more value dead or alive? Consider Naomi's plight. If she doesn't get this child, all hope for her restoration is completely gone. Without this child she is as much an outsider as Ruth was before her marriage to Boaz. If this child were "killed," there would be no continuance for Elimelech's line. That name would cease from the records. It would all be over, and the enemy would have won. Naomi truly is in the fight of her life.

Is it so farfetched to think that someone would want to kill this innocent little kinsman-redeemer? Before Moses was born, Pharaoh tried to kill all the male babies, and ended up raising and educating under his own roof the one appointed by God to deliver the Hebrew children. *He sought to destroy the one who in the end destroyed him.* What about another Deliverer, One named Jesus? King Herod, upon seeing the star in the sky, commissioned the Magi to go and search for "the Child." He said he wanted to go and worship Him – a lie! He wanted to destroy the Child, because the Child would destroy him. This is Satan's last stand, his final battle. He will use every tool in his heinous arsenal to destroy this Child before this Child restores Naomi (Israel), and before that eighth and final day. Satan knows that this is his last opportunity for survival. If he loses this time (and he will), he will be cast into the lake of fire, the bottomless pit. The fury of the Tribulation cannot be overemphasized.

The women continue speaking to Naomi, this time testifying about Ruth. They testify of the "complete" love of Ruth, the Moabite daughter-in-law, and proclaim that her love *exceeds* that of seven sons. We know from Hebrew numerology that seven means a full number, complete. We are fully aware of the absolute necessity of Ruth's adherence to her vow (Ruth 1:16-17) in our story, but peering forward, allegorically, into the current Church Age, do we have any idea of the importance of the true Church standing with Israel, and the ramifications if the Church were suddenly to be removed?

Recently, in a segment produced by "60 Minutes" about Jewish/Christian relations, it was reported that there is growing Jewish interest within the evangelical community, and they estimated that there are some 70,000,000 Christians actively in support of Israel.[35] With that tremendous figure in mind, what might we suppose would happen if all of these "supporting" Christians were instantly removed? What nation or people group would then stand with Israel? In what posture would Israel find herself? Would it be similar to the time in the wilderness when the enemy was behind her, in front of her, and on both sides of her? If the Church were suddenly taken away, would Israel's sole support be God and God alone? I believe God longs to be for Israel that Faithful Husband, Protector, Comforter and Provider. With the rapture of the Church, and the transference of the Gift of the Holy Spirit from the Church to Israel, He, indeed, will be All Israel has and All she needs.

In this same vein, and looking at this phrase, *which is better to thee than seven sons*, consider Ruth's love and devotion to Naomi, and contrast that with what her absence will mean. This verse alludes to two extremes: the depth of the love of Ruth (better than seven sons); and the depth of the mourning for Naomi when Ruth is taken away. If Ruth, indeed, is equated to seven sons (and more), then to what must Naomi's grief be likened at Ruth's death?

How unimaginable must be the mourning of a son, or two sons, or maybe even three! I'll never forget as a young girl watching an old black and white movie entitled "The Fighting Sullivans." This was based on a true story about five brothers who were killed in World War II. Mourning of that magnitude is beyond comprehension. This phrase in verse 15 not only shows the depth of Ruth's (the Church's) love, but also the inexpressible void at her absence. We are told that Israel's time of sorrow during those seven years known as The Great Tribulation will be as at no other time. There is nothing with which to compare that time – nothing!

Ruth finishes her course, she runs her race, and at the end she is declared the winner because of her selfless love, faith, humility and obedience. At a critical juncture, Ruth stepped in when Naomi stepped out. Ruth, temporarily (40 weeks in our story), kept safe the lifeline between Elimelech, Boaz and Naomi. Ruth faithfully incubated the fetus those 40 weeks, and then safely and timely delivered the long-awaited treasure.

Verse 16. ***And Naomi took the child, and laid it in her bosom,***

and became nurse unto it. What a tender verse! How genuinely exciting for us to see Naomi "taking the child" – personally getting involved – a move we haven't seen a single time this entire book. What an ugly void has filled Naomi's life from the very beginning of our story. How comforting it must be for her to hold the child ascribed to her husband, Elimelech, the gift that cost Boaz his all, the gift that took her "daughter-in-law." What an expensive treasure Naomi draws to herself. We know Naomi (Israel) has been in this role before. As a matter of fact, she's been here two other times: with her first son, Mahlon, (the Judges) and her second, Chilion (the Kings). What kind of "mother" was she in those days? Did she somehow miss valuable opportunities? Was there an independent, selfish streak about her that always insisted on having her own way? Was she more concerned with status and appearance and passing those traits on to her two "sons?" Was she only comfortable operating where she could "see?" Was the thought of walking by faith (obey first, understand later) ridiculous to her? As she holds this child, her link to Elimelech, her miraculous second chance, does she vow never again to let go, never again to do it her way, never again to be separated from the One who chose her above all others (Deuteronomy 14:2)?

> *"For thou art an holy people unto the Lord thy God, and the Lord hath chosen thee to be a peculiar people unto himself, above all the nations that are upon the earth."*

God has an amazingly lofty design for these two ladies, Naomi (Israel) and Ruth (the Church), and we dare not second guess His genius. Naomi gave up her rightful place, as the wife of Boaz, to Ruth, affording Ruth, the *nobody*, the *outsider*, membership into the most prestigious of all families. In return, Ruth gave up her rightful place as the mother of this child, affording Naomi, the *nobody*, the *outsider*, reentrance into the most prestigious of all families. We make mistakes, but God never makes a single mistake. This is His design, His strategy, and we dare not point an arrogant finger, or raise the ugly head of boastfulness or conceit! This is The Master's Plan.

After Naomi, by faith, takes the child (Holy Spirit), she then lays him in her bosom. The Hebrew meaning for this action is that she enclosed the child, she placed him in her midst, she held him within. In the allegorical realm, what do we make of this gesture? I believe the transference of this child from Ruth to Naomi had the same results as it did when it was first transferred from Jesus to the Church.

In Act 2:1-4, we read what happened at the first giving of the Gift at the time of Shavuot (Pentecost).

> *And when the day of Pentecost was fully come, they were **all** with one accord in one place. And suddenly there came a sound from heaven as of a rushing mighty wind, and it filled **all** the house where they were sitting. And there appeared unto them cloven tongues like as of fire, and it sat upon each of them. And they were **all** filled with the Holy Ghost, and began to speak with other tongues, as the Spirit gave them utterance.*

In that location in Jerusalem, a thrilling, priceless Gift was transferred to the bride of Christ. She was miraculously infused with the Spirit of the Bridegroom. This was her personal Treasure that would sustain her until the day when she and her Bridegroom were reunited. As Paul says in Philippians 1:6,

> *Being confident of this very thing, that he which hath begun a good work in you will perform it until the day of Jesus Christ.*

This Gift is the Church's Surety, her "Deed of Trust," her Pledge, her Covering until...

If that described the first giving of the Gift (the Holy Spirit), then how might we expect this same Gift to pass from Ruth (the Church) to Naomi (Israel)? Could it be in the exact same manner – with a sound from heaven as a rushing, mighty wind? (Could this be the rapture?) Will that gift fill **all** the House of Israel, as it did **all** that house that day in Jerusalem? Will there be visible tongues of fire sitting on the heads of all in "that" house? Will all be filled with the Holy Spirit and begin speaking with other tongues? If the first gifting were incredibly magnificent, how could we expect anything less of the second? Let's look at what Paul says in Romans 11 (25-26a) about the future restoration of Israel.

> *For I would not, brethren, that ye should be ignorant of this* **mystery**, *lest ye should be wise in your own conceits; that blindness in part is happened to Israel, until the* **fulness** *of the Gentiles be come in. And so* **all** *Israel shall be saved.*

When the Holy Spirit came to believers that day in Jerusalem, **all** in *that house* were saved. That was an exhilarating beginning for the Church. What Paul tells us here in Romans is that there is a new day also coming for Israel, a day in which **all** the "House" of Israel will be saved. When the Church reaches maturity (fulness), and the Gift is passed from the Church to Israel, then **all** Israel will be saved.

Let's continue in Paul's writings (Romans 11:26b-32) for a deeper look at that time.

> *...as it is written, There shall come out of Zion the Deliverer, and shall turn away ungodliness from Jacob: For this is my covenant unto them* (Israel), *when I shall take away their sins. As concerning the gospel, they* (Israel) *are enemies for your* (the Church) *sakes: but as touching the election, they* (Israel) *are beloved for the fathers' sakes. For the gifts and calling of God are without repentance. For as ye* (the Church) *in times past have not believed God, yet have now obtained mercy through their* (Israel) *unbelief: Even so have these* (Israel) *also now not believed, that through* your (the Church) mercy *they also may obtain mercy. For God hath concluded them all* (Israel and the Church) *in unbelief, that he might have mercy upon all* (Israel and the Church).

Paul says that at one time, we were *all* in unbelief in order that God might have mercy on *all*. This is the *mystery* of God. Israel for a time was moved over so that the Church could obtain mercy. Then, in the fullness of time, and through the mercy of the Church, Israel will move back into position. Israel gave place to the Church, who, in turn, will give place to her. Do you see how beautifully this is played out in the Book of Ruth? Naomi moved over, becoming a "nobody," so Ruth could become the "somebody." Then, through the selflessness of Ruth, Naomi received her "somebody" status once again.

What does it mean in Ruth 4:16 when it says that Naomi "became nurse" unto the child? The word "nurse" in Hebrew means, "turned to the right, trusted, *believed*, become steadfast, sure." Hallelujah! The one attribute for which Ruth was so blessed (her faith) is now the attribute of Naomi. By faith Naomi *personally* takes the child, lays him in her lap – in her inmost part – and becomes nurse unto him. She believes!

Verse 17. *And the women her neighbours gave it a name, saying, There is a son born to Naomi; and they called his name Obed: he is the father of Jesse, the father of David.* In this verse the child is named, therefore, we know we have reached the eighth and final day. Circumcision and naming occur on the eighth day. Naomi has made it. The women declare on this day of celebration, this victory day, the day when her mourning is complete and the child's position established, that "Naomi has a son." The Hebrew text literally reads, "he was born son to Naomi." Isn't that incredible? How could that be?

Let me tell you a very interesting story that may help you understand how we could have such a "turn of events." I have a close Israeli friend who had a child by her first husband. They divorced while the child was quite young, and she later met and married her present husband, who raised this child as his own. Years after their marriage, they moved to America, and when the child turned 16 and was ready for a driver's license, it seemed they could not get it without using the birth father's name on her license because she had never been legally adopted. She had never used that name at school, or anywhere else, so the family did not want this name on her driver's license. They returned to Israel, the land of their citizenship, to have the child legally adopted. Upon returning back to America, my friend came by our house on her way to put the adoption papers in the lock box. She was standing at my kitchen counter looking at the papers, and said to me, "I want you to look at this." I looked over her shoulder at the legal papers, all in Hebrew. She said, "An adoption in Israel is a most amazing thing. When a child is adopted, literally a new *birth certificate* is issued, and it says that the adopting parent was the parent *at the time of birth*. Legally, he or she was there *from the very beginning*. Not only that, but all prior records are removed so there is no trace of the biological parent on the record books." Stunned, I couldn't help but ask her several times to repeat it to make sure I had understood exactly what she was saying. (By the way, she was an attorney in Israel; she knows the law.)

While she was telling me this, everything inside me was shouting for joy. The Bible says we are born with a sinful nature. We were the children of Adam, but when we believe we become the children of the Living God, and we receive a newly-issued "birth certificate" that says our Father was there from the very beginning! Hallelujah!

Here in our verse, it says this child was "*born* son to Naomi," as though Ruth had nothing to do with it. I believe what we have in this verse is not only the circumcision, and the naming, but also a legal adoption. Do you recall earlier in this chapter, in verse fifteen, where it was said that this child would be a "restorer" of Naomi's life? We said that meant the ability to "turn back time, but not necessarily to the starting point." If the child restores *her* life, then who's really being adopted? Is it the child, or is it Naomi? Who's really the one out of place, and who's really the one with authority? Does Naomi have any right to adopt this child? Is it the child that establishes her position, rather than her establishing his? This adoption, indeed, restores Naomi's place in Elimelech's line, because she is holding "Elimelech's *son*," the son "born to her." What an incredible mystery! The magnitude of the role of this child is that he is able to make for Naomi a restoration that views her as having been there from the very beginning, as though she never moved over. What a superlative gift from Boaz, a timeless treasure! Also, it is of interest to note that Boaz gave the son who was attributed to Elimelech, and Ruth gave the son who was attributed to Naomi. God made a way where there seemed to be no way!

The name given this child was Obed, meaning *"servant,* in its full form possibly *servant of the Lord."*[36] In our literal story, Obed "served" both Ruth and Naomi by doing for each of them what they could not do for themselves. This child brought Ruth into the most prestigious of all "kingly" lines, and reestablished Naomi to her rightful position – directly under Elimelech. This verse goes on to say that Obed was the father of Jesse, who was the father of (King) David. What an incredible royal lineage! Obed was the child given to insure that Elimelech's line (the Messianic line) was unbroken. Elimelech's name means, "to me shall kingship come." David was the greatest earthly king who ever lived. With this gift, Elimelech's name comes to fruition.

But, it doesn't end there. God promised David (grandson of Obed) in II Samuel 7:16:

> *And thine house and thy kingdom shall be estab-lished for ever before thee: thy throne shall be estab-lished for ever.*

It was foretold to David that One from his line would *forever* sit enthroned in Israel. This was the promise of Messiah coming from David's seed. Obed, "servant" or "servant of the Lord," was a vital part of the fulfillment of that prophecy. He served Elimelech, Boaz, Naomi, Ruth, the whole House of Israel. What an incomparable fulfillment of the meaning of his name!

In our parallel realm, what about the "Obed" of our day, the Holy Spirit? Is He equally such a servant? The Holy Spirit is the Gift from Jesus to all believers. Jesus said of this Gift (John 16:13-15),

> *Howbeit when he, the Spirit of truth, is come, he will guide you into all truth: for he shall not speak of himself; but whatsoever he shall hear, that shall he speak: and he will shew you things to come. He shall*

glorify me: for he shall receive of mine, and shall shew it unto you. All things that the Father hath are mine: therefore, said I that he shall take of mine, and shall shew it unto you.

Notice how the Holy Spirit serves those who are of the household of faith. He guides them into all truth. He speaks what He hears – and, remember, He's of the heavenly realm – then passes on to us the things we can't hear without Him. He reveals to us things yet future. Jesus said that the Holy Spirit would receive from Him and then show those things to us. The revered Holy Spirit is the consummate "Middle Man." He is constantly in tune with Heaven and constantly in tune with believers on earth. He brings harmony between the two. What a Servant!

Jewish scholars teach that Obed means the one "who served the Master of the Universe with a perfect heart."[37] If *Obed* (portraying the Holy Spirit) serves perfectly the Master of the Universe, and if for nearly 2,000 years, He has kept safe and in tact the Church, then, He most assuredly can do the same for Israel in her final days.

Naomi, by taking the child, laying him in her bosom and becoming nurse unto him, has come full circle. In the beginning she was the wife of kingly Elimelech with two unworthy sons, all three of whom were taken from her. She arranged the marriage of Ruth, her outsider daughter-in-law to the family's kinsman-redeemer, relinquishing her own rightful position. The worthy kinsman-redeemer far exceeded all expectations and made a way not only for the outsider but also for the one that vacated her role. At long last Naomi has made it to this the eighth day – the day of great celebration. As Ruth (the Church in the prophetic realm) has been reunited with her faithful Husband, Boaz (Jesus), so, too, I believe here Naomi (Israel) is reunited with Elimelech (God Almighty), and all are enjoying an eternal celebration that will climax all other celebrations. They are rejoicing in Sukkot, the celebration that can only come when the weary traveler reaches the longed for Promised Land.

This is the perfect time to cover the last of the three required pilgrimages to Jerusalem. In Ruth 1:22 (Chapter Four), we looked at Passover (*Unleavened Bread, First Fruits*), and the fifty days known as the "Counting of the Omer." In Ruth 4:13 (Chapter Eleven), we covered Shavuot with its costly gift given. Here, we will view the third and final holiday of Sukkot (*Tabernacles, Ingathering*). God commanded the Israelites to celebrate this holiday when all the crops (not just the grain) were fully gathered in. The Hebrew children could not properly celebrate this feast until they reached the Promised Land. You will recall it was decreed that they wouldn't arrive until a "marked occurrence" first took place. This holiday is a memorial to the time when the Israelites wandered those 40 years, and of God's faithfulness throughout the journey. As with the other two, we will look at these from the four biblical time periods: the time of the Exodus, the time of our story, the time of Christ and present-day Judaism.

At the time of the Exodus, the Hebrew children were told to celebrate the holiday of **Sukkot**[38] by constructing booths (which is the Hebrew word sukkot) similar to the ones they used those 40 years in the wilderness. They were to live in these for seven days, and on the eighth day, they were to hold a solemn assembly (Nehemiah 8:18).

Sukkot at the time of our story would have meant the birth of the male heir. After the birth, Naomi was in a *temporary* state for another seven days, waiting until the eighth day when all was official with the child (naming and circumcision) – validating her position. We said that this temporary state encompassed the time of mourning the loss of Ruth (seven days) and waiting for the naming and circumcision of the child on the eighth day.

Sukkot at the time of Jesus follows the period between the giving of the Holy Spirit and the "marked occurrence" for which we wait – the Rapture. This will culminate in a celebration in the ultimate Promised Land with our Kinsman-Redeemer. This "Ingathering" will come to pass when *all* the "harvest" is in. We long to hear that shofar sound, shed these earthly rags and put on our wedding garments, celebrating with our Bridegroom in His Father's house.

In **Present-day Judaism, Sukkot**, is a happy time celebrated in the Fall of the year. For the seven-day celebration, Jewish families may take all or part of their meals in their sukkah (singular of sukkot), and many even sleep in them. These booths are dwellings symbolic of the temporary wilderness dwellings of the Children of Israel. They are typically of simple construction, and are gaily decorated by the family, particularly young children, with fragrant greenery and fruit. It's an exciting time for families to sleep under the stars and tell the many stories of the wanderings of their ancestors and of their final arrival in the Promised Land. The climax of Sukkot is the trip to the Synagogue on the eighth day for the holy assembly. In the Synagogue the final chapter of the Law is read, followed immediately by the reading of the first chapter of the Law. They haven't reached their final destination, so the cycle begins again. One glorious day, though, there will be that final Sukkot celebration in The Eternal Promised Land. What a glorious assembly that will be for both believing Jew and Gentile.

As the Children of Israel had a specific journey, likewise, we have a specific journey. The Israelites had a daily walk, literally and spiritually, and so do we. When they started their journey, they had no idea how long it would take. The same is true for you and me. Their walk certainly didn't go according to their plans, and didn't take the route they envisioned, and most of ours don't either. Their walk didn't end until that specific "marked occurrence," which took 40 years. We now wait for our "marked occurrence." One day we, too, will cross our "Jordan," and there we'll celebrate Sukkot with the Lover of our souls in THE Promised Land. God promises for every believer an everlasting dwelling place with Him and gives us the Gift of the Holy Spirit to guide and sustain us until our faith is sight.

> 18. *Now these are the generations of Pharez: Pharez begat Hezron,*
> 19. *And Hezron begat Ram, and Ram begat Amminadab,*
> 20. *And Amminadab begat Nahshon, and Nahshon begat Salmon,*
> 21. *And Salmon begat Boaz, and Boaz begat Obed,*
> 22. *And Obed begat Jesse, and Jesse begat David.*

These are the closing verses of the Book of Ruth. There are three Gentile women represented in this genealogy: Tamar (mother of Pharez), Rahab (mother of Boaz) and Ruth. Ten family heads are listed in these verses. We began our journey in chapter one (verse 4) with our first ten (the ten years in Moab). We said "ten" is the number of human responsibility, the number of testimony, and the number for special testing. It is quite fitting that as we began this study, so we should end it.

This story is the journey, but, in actuality, it is the walk of all mankind. We all have a unique journey – our time of human responsibility (whether we accept it or not), testimony (good or bad) and times of special testing (pass or fail). God has greatly privileged us with this intimate look into the Book of Ruth, viewing the past, present and future of all humanity. All are represented on Ruth's pages.

That threshing floor scene was not exclusive to Ruth. We each have an opportunity to visit the "threshing floor." It is *our responsibility* to go there, lie down at those feet and give the proper response. No one can do it for us, and no one can make us go. It is a choice. His costly Gift – the same, indwelling Holy Spirit – He freely offers to all. I pray that we, like Ruth, will run our race well, finish our course, and one day as we stand before God (as we most assuredly will), hear Him say, *"Well done good and faithful servant"* (Matthew 25:23).

It is imperative that we never forget the one attribute for which Ruth stood out above all others, the one for which she was blessed immeasurably – her treatment of Naomi (Israel). She made a vow with the God of Israel at the very beginning of her journey that nothing, except death, would separate her from her mother-in-law. She made herself accountable only to God by saying that if she did allow anything to part the two of them, then God was to step in and deal with "her" very severely. If we, too, want to stand out above all others in God's field, if we want His commendation and His endless blessings on our lives, then we, like Ruth, must take the same stand. God longs for the Church – corporately and individually – to take our place, shoulder-to-shoulder, with Israel, refusing to budge. No matter the difficulty, no matter the cost, no matter the ridicule, He wants our unrelenting stand with Israel.

There are two decisions the Book of Ruth demands. The first is whether or not we will go to the threshing floor and give the response of total surrender to the Kinsman-Redeemer. The second is our treatment of Israel. We've been given free will from a Sovereign God. We can choose whatever course we want. We can take the easy, "logical," comfortable way out, as did Orpah, or we can choose the uncertain, possibly difficult, "illogical" walk of faith as did Ruth.

I close with one final excerpt from Paul's writings (Romans 11:33-36):

> *O the depth of the riches both of the wisdom and knowledge of God! How unsearchable are his judgments, and his ways past finding out! For who hath known the mind of the Lord? Or who hath been his counselor? Or who hath first given to him, and it shall be recompensed unto him again? For of him, and through him, and to him are all things: to whom be glory for ever. Amen.*

AFTERWORD
"A Reader"

Ruth has always been known as a love story, and so it is. But is that *all* it is? Reading it as *only* a love story allows us to leave it where we found it – on the onion skin pages between Judges and Samuel/Kings.

All Scripture is inspired by God and is profitable for instruction, for reproof, for correction, for training in righteousness (II Timothy 3:16). Man lives by every word that proceeds from the mouth of God (Deuteronomy 8:3). All means all. Every word means every word.

The secret of Ruth is now shared with her fellow Gentile believers and has lovingly "uncovered the feet" of this God inspired book. Those feet certainly convict us to walk in the new light on the path of instruction. Can you read "…and Jesse begat David," close the book and walk away unscathed? Not if you desire training in righteousness.

A love story? You bet it is! But who are the *real* lovers? This is the secret of Ruth – now uncovered. A story of unbridled, unfathomable, everlasting passion that waits longingly – pleading to be told.

Why are these, heretofore, secrets now being discovered and recorded? God's timing my friend: "for such a time as this." Ruth's time is growing short – she is in the last days.

We are long overdue for "Ruth" to stir up some jealousy (Romans

11:14); understand the rich root into which she is grafted (vs. 17) and anticipate the re-grafting of the broken branches (vs. 24).

Naomi is waiting ——

ENDNOTES

Chapter One, Ruth 1:1-2

[1] Dr. Robert Pitman, sermon, *"The Ugliest Part of the Bible,"* Kirby Woods Baptist Church, Memphis, Tennessee, February 10, 2002.

[2] See Genesis 12:10-16; Genesis 26:1-14; and Exodus 12:35-36.

[3] See Exodus 13:16; Deuteronomy 6:8; and Deuteronomy 11:18.

[4] The four passages contained in the phylactery are Exodus 13:1-10; Exodus 13:11-16; Deuteronomy 6:4-9; and Deuteronomy 11:13-21.

[5] Rabbi Meir Zlotowitz, *The Book of Ruth*, (Mesorah Publications, Ltd., New York City, NY, 1976), p. 63.

Chapter Two, Ruth 1:3-7

[6] James Strong, *The New Strong's Exhaustive Concordance of the Bible*, (Thomas Nelson Publishers, 1990), p. 63.

[7] *Vine's Complete Expository Dictionary*, (Thomas Nelson, Inc., Nashville, Tennessee, 1996), p. 622.

[8] *The International Standard Bible Encyclopedia*, (Wm. B. Eerdman's Publishing Co., Grand Rapids, Michigan, 1986), p. 560.

Chapter Three, Ruth 1:8-17

[9] *The Jerusalem Post International Division*, 6 Oholiav St., Jerusalem, Israel, 91000, June 7, 1997, p. 19.

[10] *Israel My Glory*, The Friends of Israel Gospel Ministry, Inc., 1179 Lamonesson Rd., Deptford Township, Westville, New Jersey 08093, Feb/March, 1993, p. 10.

[11] "*The Interlinear NIV Hebrew-English Old Testament*," John R. Kohlenberger III, (Zondervan Publishing House, 1987), Ruth 1:9-19, p. 147.

[12] Dan Juster and Keith Intrater, *Israel, the Church and the Last Days*, (Destiny Image Publishers, Shippensburg, PA, 1990), pp. 121, 127, 151-152, 152-153.

[13] Marvin R. Wilson, *Our Father Abraham*, (William B. Eerdmans Publishing Company, Grand Rapids, Michigan, 1989), pp. 12-13, 15, 40.

Chapter Four, Ruth 1:18-22

[14] See Deuteronomy 16:16.

[15] See Deuteronomy 16:3-4.

[16] See Leviticus 23:9-11.

[17] See Exodus 12:1-14; Leviticus 23:5; Numbers 9:1-14; 28:16; Deuteronomy 16:1-3a; 4b-7.

[18] See Leviticus 23:11.

[19] See Deuteronomy 16:5.

[20] In Deuteronomy 16:5-6, God told the Hebrew children not to sacrifice the Passover in any town except the place He chose as a dwelling for His Name, i.e. Jerusalem. However, at the time of our story, the Temple had not been built, and the Tabernacle was just North of Jerusalem at Shiloh (Joshua 18:1).

Chapter Five, Ruth 2:1-10

[21] *Great People of the Bible and How They Lived*, (The Readers Digest Association, Inc., Pleasantville, New York, 1974), p. 129.

[22] *Holman Bible Dictionary*, (Holman Bible Publishers, Nashville, Tennessee, 1991), p. 303.

Chapter Six, Ruth 2:11-23

[23] *Judaism and Christianity*, B'nai B'rith Youth Organization, Washington, D.C., 1960, pp. 3, 8, 9, 10, 28, 29.

Chapter Seven, Ruth 3:1-9

[24] The NIV Study Bible, Zondervan Bible Publishers, 1985, p. 366, Note on Ruth 1:22.

[25] Rabbi Meir Zlotowitz, *The Book of Ruth,* (Mesorah Publications, Ltd., New York City, NY, 1976), p. 110.

Chapter Eight, Ruth 3:10-18

[26] Ibid, p. 118.

Chapter Nine, Ruth 4:1-8

[27] The NIV Study Bible, Zondervan Bible Publishers, 1985, p. 33, Note on Genesis 19:1.

[28] E. P. Barrows, *Sacred Geography and Antiquities*, p. 499.

[29] Rabbi Meir Zlotowitz, *The Book of Ruth,* (Mesorah Publications, Ltd., New York City, NY, 1976), p. 128.

Chapter Ten, Ruth 4:9-12

[30] James Strong, *The New Strong's Exhaustive Concordance of the Bible*, (Thomas Nelson Publishers, 1990), p. 105.

Chapter Eleven, Ruth 4:13-14

[31] "In the Jewish calendar, we add an entire month. This is due to the fact that our calendar is based on the moon, which has 354 days in a year, while the sun year is 365 days. Since the lunar cycle loses eleven days every solar year, we need to make up for lost time, so seven times every 19 years, a thirteenth month is added to the calendar. ..." Hannah Tiferet Siegel, (The Hebrew Watchman, Memphis, Tennessee), Thursday, March 16, 2000.

[32] Rabbi Meir Zlotoitz, *The Book of Ruth,* (Mesorah Publications, Ltd., New

York City, NY, 1976), pp. xxvi, xliii, xlvii, lvii.

[33] See Exodus 23:16a; 34:22a; Leviticus 23:11-21; Numbers 28:26-31; Deuteronomy 16:9-12.

Chapter Twelve, Ruth 4:15-22

[34] Jewish Heritage Online Magazine, July 2003, www.jhom.com/topics/seven/shiva.html.

[35] WREG-TV, "60 Minutes," June 8, 2003, Memphis, Tennessee.

[36] The NIV Study Bible, Zondervan Bible Publishers, 1985, p. 370. Note on Ruth 4:17.

[37] Rabbi Meir Zlotowitz, *The Book of Ruth*, (Mesorah Publications, Ltd., 1976), p. 135.

[38] Exodus 23:16b; 34:22b; Leviticus 23:33-36a, 39-43; Numbers 29:12-34; Deuteronomy 16:13-15; Zechariah 14:16-19.

"Did you Know?" The Tribute to the Jews on our Dollar Bill

[39] Vendyl Jones, *Will the Real Jesus Please Stand?* (Priority Publications, Inc., 1983), pp. 2-19 – 2-26.

CHART #1

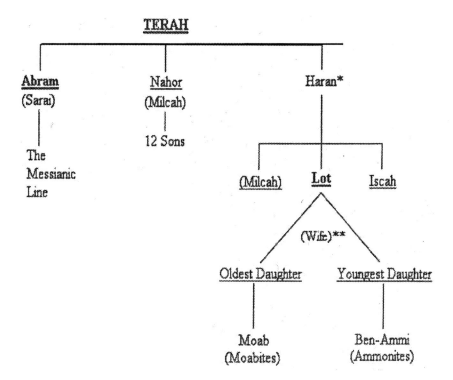

Genesis 11:26-12:4

*Haran died in Ur of the Chaldees. After Haran's death, Terah, Abram, Sarai and Lot, left Ur and settled in Haran. While there, Terah died. Then Abram, Sarai and Lot traveled to Canaan.

**Lot's wife was turned to a pillar of salt (Genesis 19:17,26). Even today, grotesque salt formations near the southern end of the Dead Sea are reminders of this event.

There's something else very intriguing about this chart. On two different occasions Abram introduced Sarai as his *sister* (Genesis 12:13; 20:2). Most commentaries believe she was his half sister. Interestingly, Nahor married his niece, Milcah, who bore him twelve sons. And, then we have the sexual relations between Lot and his two daughters. Possibly, their little "scheme" was not as bizarre in that culture as it is in ours.

CHART #2

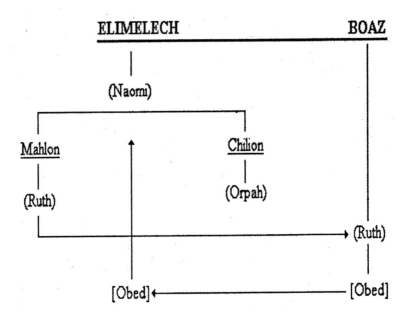

The offspring of Boaz and Ruth affirms both Ruth and Naomi.

CHART #3

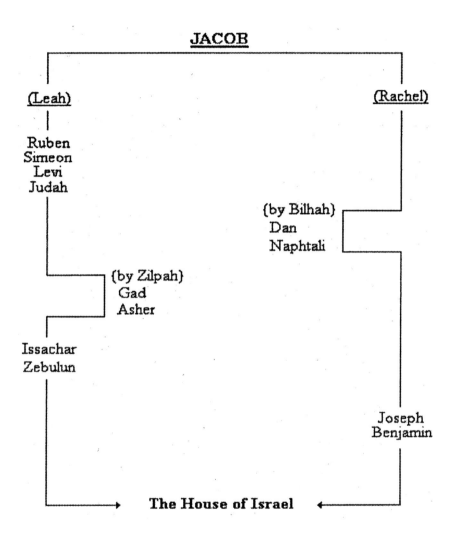

JACOB

(Leah)   (Rachel)

Ruben
Simeon
Levi
Judah

{by Bilhah}
Dan
Naphtali

{by Zilpah}
Gad
Asher

Issachar
Zebulun

Joseph
Benjamin

The House of Israel

Genesis 35:23-26 (Ruth 4:11)

CHART #4

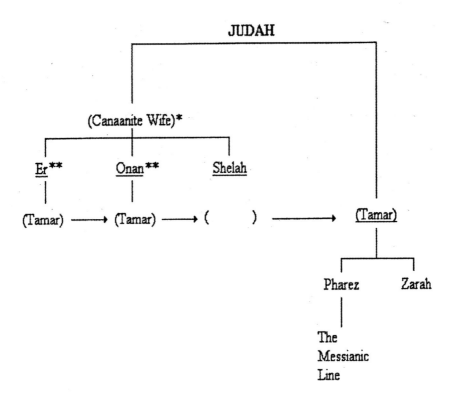

Genesis 38:1-30
*She had died.
**They were wicked, so God took them.

CHART #5

PASSOVER
FIRST REQUIRED TRIP TO JERUSALEM

Time of the Exodus	First Fruits	Counting of The Omer*
Blood Sacrifice and Death Angel passes over	Hebrews crossed Red Sea	_____ >
Time of Boaz Would have Observed Passover Meal	Boaz would have waved First Fruits offering**	____Harvests Grain____ >
Time of Christ Jesus is the Sacrifice	Jesus raised the First Fruits***	____Ascension Day 40____ >
Present-day Judaism At conclusion of Passover Meal, Jews shout, "Next Year in Jerusalem!" Signifying their hopes that The Temple will be built "next year" and they can observe Passover there.	Not observed because there is no Temple	____Formality____ >

*Leviticus 23:15; Deuteronomy 16:9.

**Barley is planted 70 days before this date in order to have the required sheaf of barley wave offering. No grain from the new crop may be eaten until after the sheaf is waved before the altar at the Temple (Leviticus 23:14). This sheaf is the tithe portion (Leviticus 23:10-11).

***I Corinthians 15:20.

(See Explanation at Ruth 1:22.)

CHART #6
SHAVUOT
SECOND REQUIRED TRIP TO JERUSALEM

Time of the Exodus		Time of Testing
The Law given*	See ** Below	_____40 years_____ >

Time of Boaz		
Kinsman-Redeemer Confronted Elimelech's Estate Redeemed Marriage to Ruth Ruth Conceives	2 Loaves Waved in the Temple	_____Pregnancy_____ > (10 Lunar Months)

Time of Christ		
The Holy Spirit (The Law) given, written on hearts and minds	Israel and Believers Waved be-Fore Altar In Heaven	_____Church Age Begins_____ >

Present-day Judaism		
Jews stay up all night Studying Torah, and the Book of Ruth	Wave Loaves not observed because there is no Temple	_____Waiting for Messiah_____ >

*Not a certainty but observed by Jews world wide as date God gave Torah, based on Exodus 19:1,11. Jewish Sages compare the giving of the Torah or Law to a "wedding between God and the Jewish people."

**Two loaves of wheat prepared from the recently harvested wheat crop, and containing leaven or yeast, are waved before the altar. (Although this command was given when the Law was given, it could not be instituted until the Children of Israel began growing crops in Canaan.)

(See Explanation at Ruth 4:13.).

CHART #7
SUKKOT
THIRD REQUIRED TRIP TO JERUSALEM
(See Explanation at Ruth 4:17)
(Feast of Tabernacles/Ingathering)

Time of the Exodus

- Sukkot was instituted as a memorial of the wilderness wanderings, and could not be celebrated properly until the Children of Israel reached the Promised Land.
- Sukkot was commanded by God to be a seven-day feast commemorating the completion of their journey, and on the eighth day, they were to hold a Holy Assembly.

Time of Our Story

- Ruth delivers baby to Naomi.
- Seven days of waiting for the naming and circumcision.
- A celebration is held on the eighth day, the day it's declared Naomi has *her* Kinsman-Redeemer, and he's given the name of Obed.
- Final chapter of the Law read, followed by the first.

Time of Christ

- Believers are looking forward to the end of our weary journey when Jesus will gather us into "The Promised Land," and the "Law" is fully complete.

Present-day Judaism

- Observant Jews eat and sleep in their sukkot (booths) for 7 days. These are temporary huts reminiscent of their "housing" during the wilderness wanderings. These booths are gaily decorated with produce and greenery, symbolizing God's bountiful harvest (Leviticus 23:41-43).

- A celebration is held at the Synagogue on the eighth day, when the final chapter of the Law is read, followed by the first, and the cycle begins again – but, one day!

CHART #8

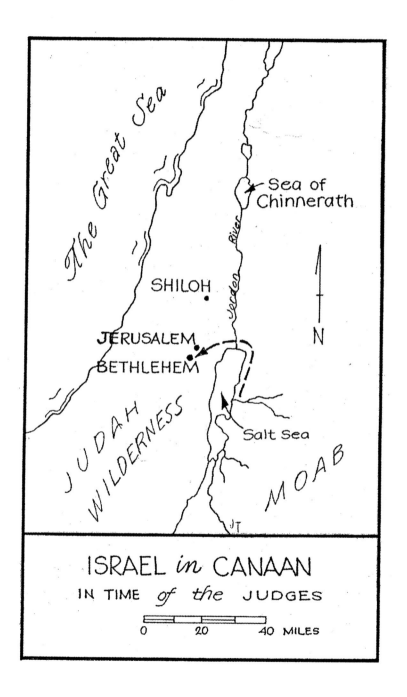

ISRAEL *in* CANAAN

IN TIME *of the* JUDGES

CHART #9
JESUS FROM GENESIS TO REVELATION

GOD'S PLAN FOR MAN'S REDEMPTION (Old Testament):
1. God created each of us to have perfect fellowship with Him (Psalm 16:11).
2. God cannot fellowship with man because of man's sin (Psalm 53:2-3; Ecclesiastes 7:20; Isaiah 59:2). This sin problem started with Adam and Eve and is still operative.
3. God will not recognize man's efforts to remove sin, "… all our righteousness is as filthy rags …" (Isaiah 64:6; cp. Jeremiah 2:22; 17:9; Micah 7:2-4).
4. God requires a blood atonement for our sins (Exodus 12:13; Leviticus 16:27, 29-34; 17:11).
5. God provided that atonement through the Messiah of Israel (Isaiah 52:13; 53:12; Zechariah 12:10).
6. God requires a personal acceptance of Messiah for salvation (Psalm 2:12; Isaiah 55:6-7; Zechariah 13:9).

GOD'S PROPHECIES ABOUT THE REDEEMER (Old and New Testaments):
A. HIS BIRTH:
   1. His lineage (Isaiah 11:1; Matthew 1:6-16; Luke 3:23-32a; Acts 13:22-23)
   2. His conception (Isaiah 7:14; Matthew 1:18-25; Luke 1:26-35)
      a. The rabbis say "virgin" (the Hebrew word almah) as used in Isaiah 7:14 always means "young woman." The same Hebrew word used in Genesis 24:43 is clearly referring to a virgin.
      b. The Hebrew word "bethula," according to rabbinic teaching, always means virgin. However, it clearly cannot be a virgin as used in Joel 1:8.
      c. The "sign" was given to the "house of David" (Isaiah 7:13), not to Ahaz.

3. His Time of Birth:
   a. Messiah was to be "cut off" 483 years after the commandment to restore Jerusalem. That order was given by Artaxerxes in 445 B.C. Reckoning the Jewish lunar calendar of 360 days, Messiah had to be "cut off" in A.D. 32 (Daniel 9:24-26).
   b. Messiah had to come and complete His redemptive work before the destruction of the Temple which occurred in 70 A.D. (Daniel 9:26).
4. His Place of Birth:
   Note that the Prophet Micah specified in which of the two Bethlehems existing at the time He was to be born (Micah 5:2; Matthew 2:1; Luke 2:4-6).

B. HIS DEATH:
   1. By crucifixion (Psalm 22:12-18; Matthew 27:34-50; John 19:28-30)
   2. Substitutionary (Isaiah 53:4-6; Daniel 9:26; Zechariah 12:10; Matthew 26:26-28)

C. HIS RESURRECTION:
   Without corruption (Psalm 16:10; 49:15; Isaiah 53:10; Matthew 27:63; Acts 2:27-31; I Corinthians 15:4-6)

D. HIS PERSON
   1. God's Son (Psalm 2:7; Proverbs 30:4; Matthew 3:16-17; Luke 1:32)
   2. Sinless (Isaiah 50:5-9; 53:11; Luke 23:4; II Corinthians 5:21; Hebrews 9:28; I John 3:5)
   3. Deity (Isaiah 7:14; 9:6; 63:8; Jeremiah 23:5-6; Micah 5:2; Zechariah 12:10; John 1:1, 14; 10:30)

E. HIS RETURN: (Zechariah 14:4-5; Revelation 19:9-16)

F. HIS NAME: "Salvation" or "Savior" (in Hebrew Yeshua or Yasha) (Isaiah 12:2; 46:13; 59:11; 62:11; Matthew 1:21)

HEBREW NUMEROLOGY

There are 22 letters in the Hebrew alphabet, and each has a number equivalency. "Aleph" is the first letter, and its number value is one; "bet" is the second, and its value is two, etc. Because each letter has numeric value, so do all words. Following are major numbers and their meanings:

1. The number one is not divisible by any other whole number. It tells of that which cannot be divided (John 17:21; Acts 4:32; Ephesians 4:1-6).

2. Two is the number of competent testimony (Numbers 14:6-8; Deuteronomy 9:15; Deuteronomy 17:6; Matthew 18:19-20; Revelation 11:3-12).

3. Three is the number of tri-unity (Ecclesiastes 4:12; I John 5:7-8; Revelation 20:10).

4. Four relates to man in connection with the earth – four seasons; four spheres: North, South, East and West; four winds of the earth; four world empires (Daniel 2:36-45; Matthew 24:31; Revelation 7:1).

5. Five is the number for God's grace. The brazen altar was five cubits in each direction. Benjamin received five times as much as his brothers. There were five loaves used to feed five thousand. David gathered five stones (Genesis 43:34; Exodus 27:1; I Samuel 17:40; Matthew 14:17).

6. Six is the number of man. Man was created on the sixth day. God gave the Israelites six days in which to do their work. There

were six cities of refuge. A bondservant was to serve six years. The number "666" is given as the number of the beast, which number is translated as the number of mankind. Six is short of perfection – man falls short of the perfect number seven (Genesis 1:26-31; Exodus 35:2; Leviticus 25:3; Numbers 35:13; Revelation 13:18).

7. Seven is the perfect number, the number of completion. It is found more times in the Bible than any other number. God created the world in seven days. Joseph foretold of seven years of feast and seven years of famine. There were seven days of consecration for Jewish priests. The blood was sprinkled before the Lord seven times. We were told to forgive seventy times seven. In Revelation, we see the seven churches, spirits, candlesticks, stars, lamps, seals, horns, eyes, thunders, heads, angels, vials, plagues, mountains (Genesis 2:2; Genesis 41:29-30; Exodus 29:30; Leviticus 4:17; Matthew 18:21-22; Revelation 1:4).

8. Eight is perfect intelligence; splendor. The digit value of "YHWH" (Jehovah) is "the Number of the Lord." The Temple was sanctified in eight days (II Chronicles 29:17).

9. Nine is the ultimate, containing the forces of all the other numbers. It refers to completion, attainment, fulfillment, regeneration and revelation (Genesis 17:1).

10. Ten is the measure of human responsibility, testimony and special testing. It also means completeness and finality. There were Ten Commandments, the parable of the ten pounds and ten days of severe persecution (Exodus 7-11; Exodus 20:1-17; Luke 19:16; Revelation 2:10).

11. The number 12 is representative of Israel. Twelve tribes, twelve apostles, the woman of the 12th chapter of Revelation (who represents Israel) with a crown of 12 stars, 12 thrones for judging the 12 tribes, the 144,000 witnesses during the tribulation: 12x12 (Matthew 19:28; Revelation 7:4-8).

12. The number 40 refers to probation and divine testing. The 40 days of rain during the time of Noah; Moses on Mount Sinai for 40 days; Israel wandered 40 years; Goliath paraded 40 days; Christ tempted 40 days (Genesis 7:12; Exodus 24:18; Joshua 5:6; I Samuel 17:16; Matthew 4:2).

13. Fifty is the number of the Holy Spirit. The Holy Spirit came

at Pentecost 50 days after the resurrection. It is the number for Jubilee, when all debts were forgiven and all slaves freed (Leviticus 27:10-11; Acts 2:1-4).

14. The number 120 (also from the number 12) speaks of that which cannot be exceeded – the extreme limit, whether of judgment or of grace. God gave the people of Noah's day 120 years to repent, there were 120 in the upper room waiting for the Holy Spirit, Solomon offered 120,000 sheep (the largest single offering ever made), the Queen of Sheba brought Solomon 120 talents of gold (Genesis 6:3; I Kings 10:10; II Chronicles 7:5; Acts 1:15).

"Did You Know?"

THE SABBATH

In Judaism the Sabbath is a very important day. As a matter of fact, Scripture refers to it as a "holiday." In the Biblical account of creation, the day began in the evening, therefore, the Jews reckon their days beginning at sundown. In Genesis 1:5 we read,

> *"... and the evening and the morning were the first day."*

The Sabbath starts at sundown on Friday and ends at sundown on Saturday.

It is interesting to note that some feast days (such as Yom Kippur, the Day of Atonement) are not only a holiday, but are also considered a Sabbath. (See Leviticus 23:26-32.) Therefore, if Yom Kippur falls on, say, a Wednesday, then that particular week will have two Sabbaths.

The Sabbath is the only day in the Bible that is named. The other days are numbered according to their relationship to the Sabbath, for instance, the "first" day of the week (the first day after the Sabbath), the "second," and so on.

A customary greeting for the Sabbath is, "Shabbat Shalom!" (SHA BAHT SHA LOME) (Shabbat is Hebrew for Sabbath.) I've never met a Jewish person that didn't appreciate my acknowledging their Sabbath in this way. If you have Jewish coworkers, it would be appropriate for you to say, upon leaving work on a Friday, "Shabbat Shalom!" (And, don't be surprised if you hear it said back to you.)

In Exodus 31:16, we read,

> *"Wherefore the children of Israel shall keep the sabbath, to observe the sabbath throughout their generations, for a perpetual covenant."*

They were commanded to honor this day *forever* (Exodus 31:12-17). This command has never been rescinded.

In the typical Jewish home, 18 minutes before sundown (because the word "life" in Hebrew has a numeric value of 18), a female – usually the mother – will light two candles. These candles are symbolic of God telling them to (1) Remember the day, and (2) Keep it holy. With her head covered (as a sign of reverence), she will light the candles, and with a circular motion, fan the fragrance of the light into her nostrils and recite this Hebrew blessing: *"Baruch atah Adonai Elohenu Melekh ha-olam, asher kidshanu b'mitzvotav v'tzi-vana l'hadleek ner shel Shabbat."* This translates, "Blessed art Thou oh Lord, King of the universe, who has set us apart by your commandments and has commanded us to kindle the Sabbath lights." (Incidentally, in the Jewish home, these candles are not extinguished, but allowed to burn out.) Next, the father pronounces a similar Hebrew blessing over the wine, and then another over the special Sabbath bread known as "challah." Oftentimes, he speaks additional blessings over his wife and children. The festive Sabbath meal follows.

In Judaism the Sabbath is a very exciting, happy day. The actual meaning for the word Sabbath is "to cease" or "to rest." Therefore, no work is done. The mother will have thoroughly cleaned the house, prepared the food and taken care of all other details so she can relax and delight in the day. One Jewish friend told me that her mother and her mother's sisters always got together before the Sabbath and cooked for hours. It was a fun time for the women to be together, and the children grew up sensing the importance, joy and excitement of the day. Also, because the Sabbath meal is a special time, often the best linens, dishes and silverware are used.

The family goes to Synagogue on the Sabbath – either Friday evening or Saturday morning. As the day is to be a day of joy, they will not only have the festive meal, but family time. There might be games, reading together, and I was even told by one Jewish friend that because it is a day of joy, many husbands and wives have intimate relations on the Sabbath.

Once I made a loaf of challah bread for a dear friend and took it over to her home late on Friday afternoon. She met me at the door, and was thrilled to have the fresh-baked bread. I kept noticing that her eyes were twinkling and seemed to be dancing, and I said, "You look excited about something." She looked around the corner of the carport at the western sky and said, "I am; it's almost the Sabbath." I have to tell you, at that moment there was a slight tinge of jealousy in me, because I didn't understand the love of this day as she did.

Ken and I had the privilege of going to Israel in 1996, and while in Jerusalem we stayed in a "kosher" hotel. Because some Jews are extremely concerned about what is and what is not work, some will not even turn on or off a light switch during the Sabbath. In our hotel, if you so chose, you could press a main button in your room that would put all the switches in both your bedroom and bathroom on a timer for the Sabbath. They would come on and go off at set times. Also, at sundown on Friday, the elevator in our hotel went on automatic and ran non-stop, opening and closing at every floor, for the 24 hours of the Sabbath. A person could get on and off without ever having to push a button.

"Did you Know?"

KOSHER

The Hebrew word kosher means "right, proper or fit to eat." There are two schools of thought on keeping kosher.

(1) *Biblical Kosher* is observed by those who follow only the commands set forth in the Torah (the first five books of the Bible.) They eat only foods specifically listed as clean in the Bible, and prohibit eating meat with the blood in it (Genesis 9:4; Leviticus 11; and Deuteronomy 14:1-21).

(2) *Rabbinic Kosher* or *Kashrut* (KAHSH ROOT), sometimes referred to as *Traditional Kosher*, is a much more complicated system with varying levels that have evolved over thousands of years. In addition to the requirements set forth in Biblical Kosher, those who observe Rabbinic Kosher do not permit the mixing of meat and dairy products together at a meal, and require that animals be slaughtered by kosher butchers in kosher slaughterhouses.

Below is a list of clean and unclean creatures recognized by both sects:

CLEAN CREATURES

4-Footed (cloven hoofed and chewing the cud): cow, deer, goat, ox, sheep

Birds: goose, chicken, duck, pigeon, quail, swan, turkey

Fish (must have fins and scales): bass, cod, flounder, goldfish, trout, salmon, tuna

Insects, etc. (winged, hopping, with four legs): cricket, grasshopper, locust

UNCLEAN CREATURES

4-Footed: camel, cat, dog, horse, rabbit, squirrel, pig

Birds: bat, crow, eagle, hawk, ostrich, owl, vulture

Fish: catfish, clams, crabs, lobster, oysters, shark, shrimp

Insect, etc.: All others not listed under "clean"

Foods prepared according to kosher standards and sold in stores are labeled on the container for the consumer. There are many different kosher symbols. Below is just a small sampling:

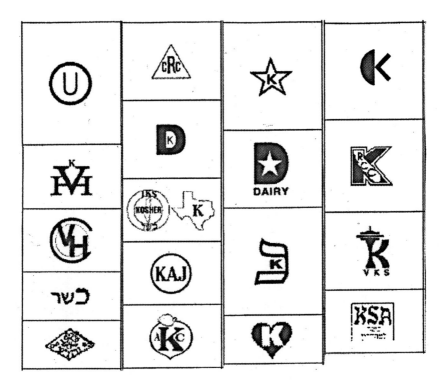

In addition to the kosher symbol, a kosher item might also indicate a "d," "m," "k-p," or "parve." The "d" means that the kosher

item contains dairy, the "m" notes products containing meat, and "k-p" signifies the item is kosher for Passover. (At Passover it is commanded that all leavening agents be removed from the house. So, these particular items are in keeping with Passover requirements.) "Parve" means the item contains neither dairy nor meat.

Leviticus 17:11, says:

> *For the life of the flesh is in the blood: and I have given it to you upon the altar to make an atonement for your souls: for it is the blood that maketh an atonement for the soul.*

This verse states that the blood is to be used for atonement, and, therefore, it is forbidden as a food. It is a major concern for Jews when some Christian groups teach that they are literally drinking the blood of Jesus when taking communion or observing the Lord's Supper. The Jews say, "I could never do that. It's forbidden." The drinking of the wine or juice in the cup is *symbolic* of our acceptance of the blood of Jesus as the atonement for our sins. It is not the literal blood of Jesus.

The way an animal is killed determines whether or not it is kosher. The process is performed by a "shochet" who first trains as an apprentice by rabbinical authority. The knives are extremely sharp and are sharpened with each use. The shochet's cut is so swift that the animal never feels pain. The jugular and the surrounding nerves are cut, and the animal dies within 2-3 seconds. The heart continues pumping, thus helping pump the blood out of the body. Kosher slaughterhouse methods are so sanitary and effective that they are exempt from many USDA regulations.

Once, I asked a dear, Jewish friend why God would tell us, for instance, not to eat shrimp. Her simplistic answer was, "Did you know that a shrimp uses the bathroom (her exact words) in his shell all his life, and it's never cleaned out?" Then I asked her why God would tell us not to eat pork. She said, "A pig will eat anything – snakes, rats, flies." But, I was reminded by another Orthodox Jew that the bottom line is, they don't eat these foods because God told them not to.

Pigs are overeaters; they never know when to quit; consequently their stomach acids are diluted because they can't keep up with the volume. This allows all kinds of parasites, bacteria, viruses and toxins to pass into the flesh of the pig, which is the part eaten. Pigs are good incubators for toxic parasites and viruses. These diseases never make them ill. The 1940 "Yearbook of Agriculture" reported finding 50 diseases in pigs that could be passed on to humans if eaten. I once heard a believing Jewish man say to a group of Christians, "You're not going to Hell for eating pork, but you may get to Heaven sooner."

Shellfish are bottom dwellers and are used to clean the ocean or fresh water floors. They are little aquatic vacuum cleaners – they take in what other fish discard. Shellfish are good and pigs are good – good to keep the food supply clean for human consumption.

In Rabbinic Kosher (Kashrut or Traditional), meat and dairy are never mixed. Deuteronomy 14:21 says,

"… Thou shalt not seethe a kid in his mother's milk."

For this reason, many Jews have two separate kitchens, including dishes, cookware, dishwashers, etc. They will go to great lengths to keep dairy and meat separate.

While we were in Israel, we stayed at a kosher hotel, and I was amazed at how they handled the meat and dairy restriction. For breakfast we had dairy and no meat – yogurt, milk, butter, cream, etc. But, for dinner, when meat was served, we had margarine, non-dairy creamer, etc.

Once, Ken and I had an "observant" (which means he keeps kosher) Jewish houseguest from Israel. I was trying to be extremely careful in preparing the meals, and chose to serve chicken at dinner and no dairy. He informed me that when fish or chicken is served (meat or fish where the mother does not nurse the young – or produce milk), it is permissible, according to *his* beliefs, to mix meat and dairy. (Although, another dear friend, who was raised orthodox, informed me that chicken was, indeed, considered meat and was never mixed with dairy in her home.) If in doubt, ask. I've never found a Jewish person yet who was offended by sincere questions.

"Did you Know?"

MEZUZAH

Y ou will find on the doorpost of Jewish homes a small case commonly known as a mezuzah (MA ZOO ZAH), which is the Hebrew word for "doorposts." In Deuteronomy 6:9, G-d commanded the Jewish people to write the following on their doorposts:

> *Hear, O Israel: The Lord our God is one Lord: And*
> *thou shalt love the Lord thy God with all thine heart,*
> *and with all thy soul, and with all thy might. And*
> *these words, which I command thee this day, shall be*
> *in thine heart: And thou shalt teach them diligently*
> *unto thy children, and shalt talk of them when thou*
> *sittest in thine house, and when thou walkest by the*
> *way, and when thou liest down, and when thou risest*
> *up. And thou shalt bind them for a sign upon thine*
> *hand, and they shall be as frontlets between thine*
> *eyes. And thou shalt write them upon the posts of thy*
> *house, and on thy gates* (Deuteronomy 6:4-9).

This passage is called the "Shema" (SHAH MAH), which is the Hebrew word for "hear," because hear is the first word in this Scripture. The words of the Shema are written on a tiny parchment paper scroll, along with the words of a companion passage (Deuteronomy 11:13-21). On the back of the tiny scroll is the Hebrew word "Shaddai." The scroll is then rolled up and placed in the case so that the first letter of Shaddai is visible on the outside of the parchment when inserted in the case.

The case and scroll are then nailed, or affixed, to the right side doorpost at an angle, with the top of the case facing the doorway. Why the angle? I was told it was because the rabbis could not decide whether it should be placed horizontally or vertically, so they compromised.

Did you notice in the first paragraph the way G-d was written? Did you think it was a typo? Many Jews will only write the words G-d or L-rd if they omit the "o," as a sign of their unworthiness to write The Holy Name. Also, there are others who, when speaking or writing about G-d, will only use the term "Ha Shem," which is Hebrew for "The Name." They won't write or say any of the names by which G-d is called.

Leonard Nemoy (Mr. Spock on Star Trek) is Jewish. Oftentimes on the show he would make a sign with his hand where his thumb was extended horizontally, and the other four fingers were opened flat and divided in the middle. This is the shape of the Hebrew letter "shin," and is a shortened version for the Name of G-d. Mr. Spock was using his hand to signify G-d's Name.

During the flight of the Space Shuttle Columbia (which ended tragically on February 1, 2003, when the craft broke apart on reentry), an article appeared in our local newspaper about Colonel Ilan Ramon, the first Israeli Astronaut. In the article, the reporter told that Colonel Ramon had taken a mezuzah aboard the space ship.

Every time a Jewish person walks through a door with a mezuzah on it, they are to touch the mezuzah and then kiss the fingers that touched it, expressing love and respect for G-d and His commandments. In the homes of the more orthodox Jews, they will have a mezuzah on the doorpost of each room in the house, with the exception of the bathroom.

"Did you Know?"

PASSOVER

What is Passover? Passover is an eight day observance commemorating the freedom and exodus of the Israelites (Jewish slaves) from Egypt during the reign of Pharaoh Ramses II. It is the oldest of the Jewish holidays, and one of three required to be celebrated in Jerusalem. The Hebrew word for Passover is Pesach (PEH SOCK).

Unique to Pesach is the eating of matzah (MAH TZAH) and the stringent prohibition of eating or possessing "chometz." Chometz is a general term for any food or drink made from wheat, barley, rye, oats, spelt or their derivatives, and is forbidden because it is leavened. Other obvious leavening agents are yeast, baking powder and soda. Leaven in Scripture is always symbolic of sin. Obvious chometz (including both food and utensils used throughout the year) should be stored in closets or rooms that are not easily accessible (locked or taped shut). In some instances, the Rabbi is called to the home to inspect the house, and if it passes inspection, he will pronounce the home "kosher for Passover." In other cases, the chometz may be sold or given to a non-Jew.

Scripture references for Passover are Exodus 12 and Leviticus 23:4-8.

The first night of Passover (and for some Jewish sects, the first and second nights), a Passover Seder (SAY DUR) is held. Seder means "order." The Seder, which lasts 2 to 3 hours, and sometimes even 4 to 5, retells the Exodus story using food for illustration: matzah represents the bread of affliction; a roasted shank bone represents the ancient sacrifice of the Passover lamb; a roasted egg symbolizes mourning for the loss of the Temple; horseradish, or "bitter herbs," symbolizes the Jews' bitter suffering under Egyptian bondage; a mixture of chopped apples, nuts, cinnamon and wine called Charoset is designed to look like the mortar used by the Jews in building the palaces and pyramids of Egypt during the centuries of forced labor; and a piece of parsley symbolizing the meager diet of the Jews in Egypt. This "telling" of the story also incorporates many songs and dances, all of which are followed by a very elaborate meal – of course, without leaven.

Personal Illustrations

- Once, a friend told me the story of how her family, while living in Poland, got rid of all the chometz in their home during Passover. She said her mother carefully cleaned all the items from the shelves and stored them in an upstairs room. When the task was complete, her father would contract with a good Gentile friend to buy that room during those eight days of Passover so that they had no chometz in *their* house. She said the transaction was legal and binding.
- Another time a friend explained to me that because you are not supposed to use the same dishes at Passover that you use all the other days (since they've had chometz in them), she gets to buy a new set of dishes every year. She said that dishes always get chipped anyway, and this is a wonderful way to get new ones. Many will even have pots and pans that are used only during the Passover season.
- Then, I had this amazing story told to me by a believing Jewish friend. She said that she really wanted to understand why God would command the Jewish people to get rid of all the leaven in their homes, so she set out on her quest. She took a week off from work, and dedicated that week to getting rid of everything

in her house that contained leaven. She cleaned the refrigerator, even pulling it out and cleaning behind it. She pulled out everything from her cabinets and pantry. She also took a toothpick and ran it in all the crevices in the corners of the cabinets getting out every crumb. She said it was very tedious, but when it was all over, she discovered why God gave the command. He wanted the people to see that by human effort, it is absolutely impossible to get every last crumb that contains leaven out of the house. (Remember, leaven in Scripture is symbolic of sin.) In the same way, it is impossible for us to get sin out of our lives. That's a God-sized task. Only He can do it. She was amazed at the conclusion to which she had come.

- Another Jewish friend told me that it was a big thing the day before Passover to have the Rabbi come over to their house and look through the cabinets, pantry, etc., and pronounce the house "kosher for Passover." She said her mother would put all the items containing leaven in one section of their shelves and cover this section with a white sheet. After the Rabbi's inspection, her family would pay him for services rendered.

- A comical story shared with me from another friend was about a family with a dog on a special diet. Because they could not change his dog food during the eight days of Passover, they had to "sell the dog" and, of course, his food along with him, until after Passover.

"Did you Know?"

THE KIPPAH
(Yarmulke or Skullcap)

The Kippah (KIH PAH) (which is Hebrew for skullcap) or yarmulke (YAR MU KAH), as it is also sometimes called, is worn by many Jewish men all the time, and by all males – Jews and non-Jews – at Jewish holy sites. It is a custom more than a commandment. During the Temple period, only the priests wore a head covering. After the destruction of the Temple in 70 AD, the Rabbis began wearing caps in the Synagogue as a sign of respect to God and His presence in the Holy Place.

A fourth century Rabbi, in reading from Isaiah 6:3,

> *"Holy, Holy, Holy is the Lord of hosts: the whole world is full of his glory,"*

determined that as God's glory is everywhere, he should wear a kippah all the time, thus began the tradition.

In ancient times an uncovered head was a symbol of freedom and human strength. So, the kippah proclaims that man is subject to God, whose hand is always over him.

Although traditionally only worn by men, today it is not uncommon to see a woman wearing a kippah during worship and prayer.

One Saturday Ken and I decided to go back "home" to the Mississippi Delta for the day and reminisce at some of our old, favorite places. We went to the town of Clarksdale, Mississippi, and Ken said, "Do you want to go see their Synagogue?" Of course I wanted to. We looked in the phone book for the address, but couldn't find the street. We asked around, and still couldn't find it. So, we went back to Main Street to ask someone at one of the Jewish stores. In front of one of these stores stood a young woman with a yarmulke on her head! I couldn't believe my eyes. That was my first time ever to see a woman wearing a yarmulke. I said, "I see someone who can surely tell us where the Synagogue is." As it turned out, she "just happened" to be the interim Rabbi. She smiled at my obvious astonishment at her head covering. One of the women standing with her graciously offered to escort us to the Synagogue. It was one of those moments never to be forgotten. I can personally attest to the fact that some women (although not Orthodox) do, indeed, wear yarmulkes or kippahs.

At the Bar and Bat Mitzvahs we've attended, the men were given a kippah to wear when entering the Synagogue and as a memento of the occasion. The young person's name was imprinted on it, and the date of the event. Also, at Jewish weddings we've attended, the wedding party provided yarmulkes with the names of the bride and groom and the date.

"Did you Know?"

THE TALLIT
Or Prayer Shawl

In biblical times Jewish men always wore a Prayer Shawl called a tallit (TAH LEET). Tallit means "tent" or "to cover." In Numbers 15:37-41 and Deuteronomy 22:12, the Israelites were commanded to wear fringes, tassels or twisted coils on the corners of their garments. In wearing these fringes, the Jewish male was to (1) remember the commandments of the Lord, and was to (2) obey them.

> *And the Lord spake unto Moses, saying, Speak unto the children of Israel, and bid them that they make them fringes in the borders of their garments throughout their generations, and that they put upon the fringe of the borders a ribband of blue: And it shall be unto you for a fringe, that ye may look upon it, and remember all the commandments of the Lord, and do them; and that ye seek not after your own heart and your own eyes, after which ye use to go a whoring: That ye may remember, and do all my commandments, and be holy unto your God. I am the Lord your God, which brought you out of the*

*land of Egypt, to be your God: I am the Lord your
God* (Numbers 15:37-41).

Tzitzit (TZEE TZEET) is the Hebrew word for tassels. Tzitzit
has a numeric value of 600. There are eight strands and five double
knots in each tassel (13) for a combined total of 613, the number of
commandments given by God to the Children of Israel on Mt. Sinai.

Jewish men often pull the tallit over their heads during morning
prayers, forming their own "prayer closet." Once I was at a synagogue service, and during prayer time I peeped (I'm glad I did). I
saw a man take his prayer shawl and reach over and cover his wife,
pulling her into his "prayer closet." It was a beautiful sight.

The writing at the neck edge of the tallit is the Hebrew blessing:

*"Blessed are thou, Lord our God, King of the
universe, who has sanctified us with His commandments and commanded us to wrap ourselves in the
tzitzit."*

Another time while shopping at a department store, I noticed a
tall, nice-looking young man come in, with a yarmulke on his head.
Because of the yarmulke, I was drawn to him, and watched him out
of the corner of my eye. As he reached up on a top shelf for an item,
I was surprised to see the fringes exposed under his shirt. If I hadn't
actually seen them, I would never have suspected that underneath
his simple, plaid shirt were the commanded tzitzit (fringes) of
Numbers 15:38. I came to understand that there are smaller
"fringes" which fit easily under street clothes (as in the case of this
young man), and, of course, the larger ones seen in Synagogues.

The tallit is worn as a way of life or tradition. It is used at all
major Jewish occasions: circumcisions, bar mitzvahs, weddings and
burials. It protects the scrolls of the Torah (the first five books of the
Bible) when they are moved; the bride and groom are covered with
the canopy of the prayer shawl, and the dead are wrapped in them
for burial. It is also the inspiration for the Israeli flag – a "tallit"
stretched out with the Star of David in the center.

The shawls in biblical times had blue threads. The blue came from dye excreted from the Chilazon sea snail. This dye was so scarce that it was worth its weight in gold, literally. It colored the robes of the kings and princes of Media, Babylon, Egypt, Greece and Rome. Since it was identified with royalty, the Romans issued an edict that only royalty could wear garments with the dye, and only imperial dye houses were permitted to manufacture it. So, the Jews had to discontinue its use, and the sea snail became extinct.

Recently, however, there has been a revival of interest in the blue dye in Israel. As a result of extensive research, and the reappearance of the sea snail, the dye is once again being produced, and threads are available for use in prayer shawls, although quite expensive.

In Matthew 9:20 when the woman with the issue of blood came up and touched the "hem of Jesus' garment," she actually touched the fringe, or the tzitzit, he wore – as commanded.

"Did you Know?"

THE ROLE OF A SCRIBE IN PRESERVING THE SCRIPTURES

The question posed in the corresponding chapter of our study in Ruth was, "When did Israel ever tell the Church how to find the Kinsman-Redeemer?" The answer is, "We were shown the way to the *Threshing Floor* through the Holy Scriptures received by Israel, penned by Israel, preserved by Israel and shared by Israel with the whole world." Luke 24:27 says,

> *And beginning at Moses* (the Torah, first five books of the Bible) *and all the prophets, he* (Jesus) *expounded unto them in __all__ the scriptures the things concerning himself.*

Let's delve a bit deeper into what it took for the Scribes to preserve the Bible. The Priests and Scribes carefully copied every word of the Scripture on Scrolls. Everything was done by hand, one Hebrew character at a time. They took every precaution to make certain that each copy was without error. They would count the actual number of letters in the master Scroll, and then count the number of letters in the completed Scroll. If they were not identical, they would destroy the copy. In copying the Scriptures, every time the Scribe came to the name of Jehovah, he would empty the ink from his pen, rinse the pen, put new ink in the pen, wash himself, and then he was ready to write the name of Jehovah. When the Name was complete, he would empty the pen again, put the old ink back in, and commence with the rest of the words. Even if the Name Jehovah was in a verse two or three times, he would go through this same process each time. They would not write that Name with the same ink with which they wrote the common words. Their important task was to preserve the Scriptures, the very Word of God, for succeeding generations – Jew and Gentile alike. They took their work seriously.

Look at the requirements in the Talmud (Jewish commentary) for copying the Scrolls:

(1) The parchment had to be made from the skin of a kosher animal, prepared only by a Jew and fastened by strings made from the skins of clean animals.

(2) Each column had to have no less than 48, and no more than 60, lines.

(3) The ink had to be of no other color than black and had to be prepared according to a precise formula.

(4) No word or letter could be written from memory. The Scribe had to have an authentic copy before him, and he had to read and pronounce aloud each word before writing it.

(5) The Scribe had to reverently wipe his pen each time before writing the word for God, and he had to wash his whole body in the mikvah, the ceremonial bath, before writing the sacred Name, Jehovah (YHWH).

(6) One mistake on a sheet condemned the sheet. If three mistakes were found on any given page, the entire manuscript was condemned.

(7) Every word and every letter was counted, and if a letter was omitted, an extra letter inserted, or if one letter touched another, the manuscript was condemned and destroyed at once.

The old Rabbis gave this solemn warning to each young Scribe: "Take heed how thou dost do thy work, for thy work is the work of heaven, lest thou drop or add a letter of a manuscript and so become a destroyer of the word." The Jews were entrusted with the very oracles of God. God chose them to be the keepers of His Word, and they kept His Word in tact with all reverence.

And, in those carefully preserved Old Testament Scriptures was the plan of salvation, the way to the "threshing floor."

(a) God created man to fellowship with Him (Psalm 16:11).
(b) God cannot fellowship with man because of his sins (Psalm 53:2-3; Ecclesiastes 7:20 and Isaiah 59:2).
(c) God will not recognize our efforts to remove sin (Isaiah 64:6; Jeremiah 2:22 and Micah 7:2-4).
(d) God requires a blood atonement for our sins (Exodus 12:13; Leviticus 16:27 and 17:11).
(e) God provided that atonement through the Messiah (Isaiah 53:1-12 and Zechariah 12:10).
(f) God requires a personal acceptance of Messiah for salvation (Psalm 2:12; Isaiah 55:6-7; and Zechariah 13:9).

In the Old Testament, God perfectly laid out His plan of redemption. Truly, Naomi (Israel) did share with Ruth (the Church) the way to Boaz (Christ), the Kinsman-Redeemer, and we should forever be grateful.

"Did you Know?"

BAR MITZVAH and BAT MITZVAH

"On Bar/Bat Mitzvah day,
a Jewish child becomes an adult,
fully responsible to God for
becoming a better person."

According to Jewish law, a boy is deemed a "bar mitzvah" and achieves the status of adulthood when he turns 13. A Jewish girl becomes a "bat mitzvah" when she turns 12 (reportedly, because girls mature earlier than boys). "Bar" means son, "bat" means daughter, and "mitzvah" means commandment; thus, they become a son or daughter of the commandment.

The celebration is observed on the Sabbath following that twelfth or thirteenth birthday, as the case may be, or shortly thereafter. Under Jewish Law children before bar/bat mitzvah age are not required to observe the commandments, although they are encouraged to do so. However, it is at this strategic milestone that they are obligated to observe the commandments, and this ceremony formally marks this requirement. To hold the service, it is necessary for a "minyon" to be present. Minyon means quorum (ten Jewish males who have reached the age of bar mitzvah).

According to one source, a Jewish male is automatically a bar mitzvah (a son of the commandment) when he reaches the age of 13. No ceremony is necessary to transfer these rights and obligations. The elaborate ceremonies, with which we in America are familiar, do not fulfill any commandment, and such celebrations were unheard of a century ago.

In its most basic form, a bar mitzvah is the young man's first "aliyah" (AH LEE YAH), which means "to go up" – as in to be invited up to the platform to read from the Torah Scroll or from the Haf Torah (the prophets). (You may also hear of Jewish people making "aliyah" to Israel, meaning they are "going up" or "moving up" to Israel.)

During the service, the young honoree will have prepared a speech that traditionally begins with the phrase, "Today I am a man." Bar mitzvah, simply stated, is the age when a person is held responsible for his or her own actions. At this service the father recites a blessing, thanking God for removing the burden of being responsible for the son's sins.

Today's celebrations of the bar/bat mitzvah here in America may be something on this order. Typically, there will be a large gathering of family, and possibly close friends, for the Friday evening Shabbat meal, which, of course, must be kosher. Invitations are sent for the ceremony at the Synagogue, which will be held either Friday evening or Saturday morning. The synagogue service is usually quite lengthy. During the service, in addition to the honoree's reading from the Torah in Hebrew (for which he's diligently studied), and making his speech, other family members will go up to the platform and also make speeches. Afterwards, there may follow a festive celebration for everyone. Saturday evening may conclude with an additional party geared more to the young people, such as a barn dance or a pool party, etc.

A new trend is traveling to Israel to hold the celebration in Jerusalem at the Wailing Wall. Needless to say, these events can be quite costly for the families. The parents of the honoree will oftentimes cover all the expenses for special relatives and guests, including travel, lodging and meals. At one Bar Mitzvah, to which Ken and I were invited, the family had installed a swimming pool for the occasion, costing some $20,000. When you add up the cost of the parties, travel expenses for so many, etc., you understand these affairs can be quite costly. One writer even noted that the receptions that follow the bar mitzvah service are often as elaborate as a wedding reception.

These events are extremely important to the Jewish families, but for Gentiles, we just don't understand. If you are privileged to receive an invitation, please make every effort to honor the family with your presence. You are invited not in order to receive a gift, but because you are a valued friend.

The appropriate greeting to the bar/bat mitzvah honoree is, "Mazl Tov" (MAH ZL TOVE), which is Hebrew for "Good Luck!" An acceptable gift is 18 new one dollar bills (a check is fine, too). Eighteen is the numeric value for "life" in Hebrew.

"Did you Know?"

THE JEWISH FUNERAL

In Judaism a funeral, traditionally, occurs within 24 hours after death. Jews do not believe in embalming. They reverence the Scripture that teaches our bodies are to be returned to dust and not preserved. Genesis 3:19, states:

"... for dust thou art, and unto dust shalt thou return."

Because decay begins immediately upon cessation of life, burial occurs within a day, or as soon as possible thereafter under extreme circumstances. Also, because the funeral service is rushed, the only means of letting others know about the death and the funeral service is by "word of mouth."

The following is my experience at an orthodox funeral, and may be of use to some of you. Funerals are personal, so each will be different, and Jewish funerals vary depending upon whether they are orthodox, conservative, reform, etc.

Upon entering the chapel for this particular orthodox service, there was a registry for names and addresses, and Siddurs (books to be used during the service). There were also appropriate head coverings for both men and women, black yarmulkes for the men and black lace circles for the women. (It is quite appropriate for everyone to use the head coverings provided – Gentiles, too.) When the service began, the family was seated, and then the casket was brought in.

The Rabbi acknowledged before the congregation the sadness of the occasion, and then went to the widow and the children of the deceased and tore a garment on each of them as a symbol of their mourning. At this particular funeral, the Rabbi tore the veil of the women and a pocket on the dress shirt of the men. The service proceeded with the Rabbi quoting Scripture, and the Cantor chanting in Hebrew. The Scriptures used were Psalm 8:4, where the Psalmist asks,

"What is man that thou art mindful of him?"

and Psalm 15:1, wherein the Psalmist asks,

"Lord, who shall abide in thy tabernacle? Who shall dwell in thy holy hill?"

The Rabbi then delivered his message, paying tribute to the deceased's many accomplishments and good deeds. The Scripture concluding the service was the 23rd Psalm.

The family and congregation then walked from the chapel to the adjoining cemetery for the burial. The family was seated in side chairs, while all others stood. The Rabbi, Cantor and pallbearers then proceeded to lower the wooden coffin into the grave. Next, they placed two concrete slabs on top of the coffin, each about six inches thick and the size of the coffin. These were to satisfy our state's legal requirement for having a vault. Then the Rabbi began shoveling dirt into the grave, followed by the Cantor, and then the pallbearers, each taking turns. It was a solemn time, with only the sounds of singing birds, passing automobiles and the dirt filling the grave.

Then a most amazing, spontaneous thing happened. An African-American gentleman (a Gentile) stepped forward and took the shovel to assist, and when he did, tears welled up in my eyes thinking of God's perfect plan for unity between Jews and Gentiles. When the grave was nearly filled, the Rabbi read more Scripture, and the Cantor chanted. Then the Rabbi cautioned all of us to go home and wash, because Scripture demands such when one touches a dead person (although none of us had touched the body). We were then asked to form two lines, the family walking between the two, receiving condolences.

A couple of obvious things I noticed were that there were no flowers. The "wooden" coffin was draped with a black cloth covering with Hebrew writing on it. I also noticed rocks placed on many of the gravestones at the Jewish cemetery. These are used as memorial stones, reminiscent of Scriptures where the children of Israel were instructed to take stones and set them up as markers so they would not forget a specific incident. You may remember at the end of the movie, "Schlindler's List," the Jews he had saved all walked past his grave and placed a rock on it. These were memorial stones. Also, almost everyone there was dressed in black, and the widow had on no makeup, and her hair was not fixed. She was outwardly and inwardly in mourning.

Back in the chapel, before dismissing us to the cemetery, the Rabbi told the congregation that the family would be "sitting sheva," giving the days (which, of course, excluded the Sabbath), and gave the address of the home. "Sheva" is the Hebrew word for seven. This means that for seven days, the family receives visitors wishing to pay their respects. Many may not have gotten word of the death in time to go to the funeral, and this "sheva" period allows friends appropriate opportunity to visit. When you visit someone sitting sheva, you will, no doubt, be told many heartwarming stories of the deceased. It is a time of fondly sharing and remembering.

On another occasion when I visited a different Jewish family who was sitting sheva, I was delighted to be taken through various parts of their home to view the many paintings and pieces of art created by the deceased. This particular person had been a television personality that I had greatly admired as a child, and I was deeply honored.

Because kosher restrictions are so rigid, and viewed differently by the different Jewish sects, it is not advisable to take any food when going to the home, even from a kosher bakery. However, fruit is always kosher and appropriate, if you feel you "must" take something, but it is not expected.

If you would like to make a memorial, one you might consider that will be genuinely appreciated is having a tree planted in Israel in memory of the deceased. There are several organizations that offer this service, and all can be found on the internet. But, here I offer one such organization that has been in existence since 1901. It is the Jewish National Fund. You can contact them either by phone at 1-888-JNF-0099, or through their web site at www.jewishnation-alfund.com. The cost to plant a tree with this organization is $18.00, and they will send notification to the family. (You will recall our earlier discussion in Hebrew numerology of "life" having the numeric value of 18. This is a very important word and number in Jewish culture.)

"Did you Know?"

MAJOR BRANCHES OF JUDAISM

The major denominations within Judaism range from the more traditional Orthodox to the more liberal Reconstructionists. There are approximately 6 million Jews living in America today that represent the Orthodox to the liberal, and the many shades in between. Following is a brief summary of each:

Orthodox Judaism is the most traditional branch of Judaism. They follow Jewish law as laid down in the Torah (the first five books of the Bible) and the Talmud (compilation of Jewish law). They believe God gave the whole Torah to Moses at Mt. Sinai, and that it has remained intact and unchanged. Some refer to them as "modern" Orthodox in order to distinguish them from the **Hasidim** (the more stringent ultra-Orthodox). The Orthodox prays 3 times a day, eats only kosher food, goes to Synagogue every Shabbat, refrains from sexual intercourse for 2 weeks each month (during the woman's menstrual cycle and seven days past), avoids inter-religious marriage, devotes much time to the study of Scripture, and nearly always sends their children to Jewish schools. Synagogue services are mostly in Hebrew, with the men and women sitting separately during services. Women are excluded from the rabbinate, from reading the Torah in the Synagogue, and a woman does not count in the required quorum of ten (known as a "minyon" in

Hebrew) to hold a prayer service. Interestingly, they (particularly the ultra-Orthodox) are expecting the imminent arrival of Messiah. There are some 1 million Orthodox American Jews, with approximately 1,200 congregations.

Conservative Judaism seeks to retain what adherents see as the essential elements of traditional Judaism but allows for the modernization of religious practices (such as holding more "practical" prayer services in which both men and women can lead), yet they are not as liberal as the Reform or Reconstructionists. Conservatives seek a middle ground approach between the Orthodox and Reform. This movement arose from tension between the two advocates. Conservative Judaism believes that while sacred Jewish writings did come from God, there was a human component, and while Jewish law should be obeyed, it must adapt. Although Conservative Jews believe changes in customs are inevitable, they believe they should be made reluctantly. Their services are held in Hebrew and English. In 1985, the Conservative Rabbinical Association approved the ordination of women rabbis. There are some 2 million Conservative American Jews, with approximately 800 congregations.

Reform Judaism is considered to be lenient, adapting Judaism to constant changes in the world. They maintain that no one formulation of Jewish belief or codification of Jewish law was meant to be eternal. They believe that while the Torah is a valuable cultural and philosophical work, it was not delivered by God at one time, but developed over centuries. Reform Jews say Judaism must continue to evolve with each individual free to decide what to believe. They conduct their services in a contemporary language, such as English, as opposed to Hebrew. In recent decades, however, there has been a tendency to return to a more traditional attitude. Their synagogues are called temples, and they favor no distinction between the sexes. They follow the spirit but not the letter of the Orthodox practices. Reform Judaism began in Germany in the 1800s. In Israel it is the Reform group that is most willing to make concessions to the demands of the Palestinians. Most Reform Jews only go to temple on the High Holy Days. There are some 1.3 million Reform American Jews, with approximately 848 congregations.

Reconstructionist Judaism is a relatively new, fast growing branch which began in New York in the 1900s. The Reconstructionist movement grew out of Conservative Judaism. They believe that Judaism is an evolving, religious civilization, and while they accept the importance of the Jewish heritage, they do not believe those practices must remain unchanged. Rather, they call for "reconstructing" Judaism, as needed to fit contemporary traditions, while maintaining the intentions of the past. It is probably the most liberal branch. It views Judaism as a constantly changing and evolving religion, and believes these changes should be embraced. It differs from the other branches in that it does not necessarily see Jews as "the chosen people." Reconstructionists are often non-Rabbi-led groups that deny original sin and uphold the basic goodness of humankind. There are some 50,000 Reconstructionist American Jews, with approximately 80 groups.

Messianic Judaism is a relatively young movement and is comprised of both Jews and Gentiles who believe Jesus is the promised Messiah. They freely welcome all beliefs and nationalities to join in their worship. They honor the Shabbat and all Biblical feast days, and most keep kosher. They do not consider themselves a "church," but rather refer to themselves as a "congregation of Jewish believers." They call Jesus by His Hebrew name, "Yeshua," (YEH SHU AH), which means salvation, and embrace both Old and New Testaments. Their services are in both English and Hebrew, always reading from the Torah Scrolls in Hebrew.

"Did you Know?"

CIRCUMCISION

The circumcision, in Hebrew the Brit Milah (BRIT ME LAH) (also sometimes called Bris) is one of the most fundamental precepts of the Jewish religion. The correct procedure has not changed since Abraham performed this covenant over 3,500 years ago. Ritual circumcision is a sign attesting to the everlasting covenant God established with the Jewish people through Abraham in Genesis 17, and reiterated to Moses 500 years later,

> *"And in the eighth day the flesh of his foreskin shall be circumcised,"* (Leviticus 12:3).

Circumcision is performed by a mohel who has special training in the medical and surgical techniques. The mohel is usually a rabbi, cantor or other spiritual leader who understands, upholds and practices the tenets of the Jewish religion, and is specially trained to function as such. The procedure involves the removal of a small piece of skin; no flesh or muscle is cut when correctly done. It is considered almost painless, and takes 10-15 seconds. There is minor discomfort for about four to six hours, and complete healing in two to three days. (I am told that where no mohel is available, an observant, Jewish medical doctor will be called to perform the procedure. It will be done in the same manner as the mohel, which is different from the medical procedure in hospitals.)

A brief description of the ceremony is as follows: The parents enter with the baby, and place him on a chair known as "the Chair of Elijah." The baby is then placed on the lap of a designated person (most often a grandfather) who holds the baby during the procedure. After the appropriate blessing is recited, the circumcision is performed by the mohel. Immediately following the Bris, another blessing is said over a cup of wine, and the baby receives his official Hebrew name.

> *"And when eight days were accomplished for the circumcising of the child, his name was called JESUS, which was so named of the angel before he was conceived in the womb,"* (Luke 2:21).

The ceremony ends with the resounding wish of "Mazel Tov" (MAH ZL TOVE – Good Luck)! The entire observance lasts approximately 15 minutes. Serving of refreshments or a light meal usually follows. It is customary to have a minyon (at least 10 adult men – those over the age of 13) present. The traditional gift is money that will go toward the child's Jewish studies.

Even if an infant dies before he is circumcised, he is to be circumcised at the gravesite. And, if a father fails to have a son circumcised, after the child becomes an adult (13), he is obligated to see that the commandment is fulfilled.

The ceremony is performed on the eighth day, if the child is healthy. It is interesting to note that modern medicine (only in the past 15 years) has discovered that the eighth day is the best day for the procedure because Vitamin K, the clotting factor, is at its highest level – higher than on the seventh, ninth or tenth day. (Babies circumcised in the hospitals before going home ((usually the second day)) are given injections of Vitamin K.) After the procedure, the severed skin is customarily buried in earth or sand.

The circumcision of a Jewish male is an extremely momentous occasion because it is a sign of being in a covenant relationship with God. No uncircumcised male was allowed to speak in the Temple.

"Did you Know?"

THE TRIBUTE TO THE JEWS ON OUR DOLLAR BILL

A personal friend of George Washington called on him with a proposal for an American revolution against the mighty British Empire. To show his sincerity, the friend offered his entire fortune, 600,000 British sterling, to begin the American Revolution.

Haym Salomon did far more than put his own fortune into the American Revolution. He made a trip to France and met with his business associates, the Sassoons and Rothschilds, who raised an additional three and one-half million British sterling to finance the American cause.

Haym Salomon also solicited every able-bodied Jewish man to volunteer to fight with Washington's army. Many Jews fought in the American Revolution and soon afterward organized the first American veterans' organization, "The Jewish War Veterans."

The first draft of the Constitution and the Great American Seal were submitted by Haym Salomon. Salomon's Constitutional draft was rejected. As to the American Seal, a committee of Franklin, Jefferson and Adams was appointed to come up with a simpler, more acceptable seal of state. After several years of quibbling, Haym Salomon's seal was approved with some modifications.

Haym Salomon saw the American Revolution as the eagle breaking away from the lion of Great Britain. He used the symbol as the signet of the master confederacy of the United States.

To the Jews, thirteen is the number of perfect unity. There were thirteen tribes of Israel (Joseph's two sons, Manasseh and Ephraim, took his place). A Jewish boy has his Bar Mitzvah at age thirteen. Seven times each nineteen years, the Jewish calendar has thirteen months. These seven years with thirteen months keep the lunar calendar in perfect unity with the solar system. Now, notice the thirteen leaves on the olive branch in the eagle's right talon, the thirteen arrows in his left, the thirteen stripes on the shield on the eagle and the thirteen stars in the cloud, representing the thirteen colonies.

Look closely at the shape of the five-pointed stars, and you will note they form the Star of David. This star was on David's shield, but it did not originate with David. Tradition has it that the Jewish star goes all the way back to the exodus from Egypt in the Jewish year 2448.

Now, look at the Seal upside down. Cover the eagle's head with your thumb, and the shield becomes the menorah, or seven candlesticks, of Israel's spiritual economy and the official Seal of State for Modern Israel. (The Star of David is the national seal of Israel's political economy, while the seven golden candlesticks, or menorah, represent Israel's spiritual or religious economy.)

Cover the shield completely, and you see the nine-feathered tail, representing the nine flames of the Hanukkah Menorah.

In the right talon of the eagle is the olive branch. Since Noah's flood, it has been the plant symbol for mercy and peace in Israel. In the left talon are the arrows, symbols of judgment and war.

Every Gentile who ever carried a dollar bill with Haym Salomon's seal has a little reminder of the American prosperity.[39]

> *"... I will bless them that bless thee* (Israel), *and curse him that curseth thee: and in thee shall all families* (Jew and Gentile) *of the earth be blessed"* (Genesis 12:3).

Do we owe a debt of gratitude to the Jews? Absolutely! And, we should thank God that George Washington had us all remember?

$$\begin{array}{r} 300 \\ 122 \\ \hline 478 \end{array}$$

Printed in the United States
34793LVS00004B/64-510

9 781597 813389